APPROPRIATING LITERACY

Appropriating Literacy
Writing and Reading in English as a Second Language

Judith Rodby

Boynton/Cook
HEINEMANN
Portsmouth, NH

BOYNTON/COOK PUBLISHERS
A Subsidiary
HEINEMANN EDUCATIONAL BOOKS, INC.
361 Hanover Street   Portsmouth, NH 03801–3959
Offices and agents throughout the world

Copyright © 1992 by Judith Rodby.

Library of Congress Cataloging-in-Publication Data
Rodby, Judith.
    Appropriating literacy : writing and reading in English as a
second language / Judith Rodby.
        p.   cm.
    ISBN 0–86709–308–0
    1. English language—Study and teaching—Foreign speakers.
2. Literacy programs. I. Title.
PE1128.A2R586   1992
428'.007–dc20   92–18835
                                                                CIP

Printed in the United States of America
92 93 94 95 96 9 8 7 6 5 4 3 2 1

For Tom

Contents

Acknowledgments

The ideas in this book have developed over many years. They were nurtured by my friends and mentors in the Rhetoric, Linguistics and Literature Program at the University of Southern California: W. Ross Winterowd, Stephen Krashen, Teresa McKenna; also, Chapter 5 owes much to Michael Holzman, Chapter 6 to Louise Wetherbee Phelps; thanks to Elspeth Stuckey for the many hours of conversation on these topics, and to Marilyn Cooper who has continually helped me to refine my ideas and my prose.

My colleagues and students at California State University, Chico, have also been enormous support, reading and commenting on the drafts of this manuscript: thanks to Tom Fox for invaluable insights and consistent willingness to read my work, and to Tricia Lord for her encouragement, her great ear, and especially for her work with Roxana Jovel. Thanks for perceptive comments on Chapters 1 and 2 to Stuart Koster, Julie Leigh, and John Marble. This book was completed with the help of a California State University research grant. I want to thank Professor Carol Burr, and Dean Donald Heinz, who supported my grant applications.

For their patience and good humor, thanks to Tom, Siobhan, and Maura Barrett.

Introduction

Novelists composing in Nigeria, Chicano poets reading their work in Wisconsin, future engineers from Malaysia studying in Texas, migrant workers attending adult education classes in California—such is the diversity of contemporary writing and reading in English as a Second Language. As these readers and writers appropriate literacy in English, teachers and administrators are pressured with growing and evolving expectations for ESL literacy and composition classes.[1] In this volatile atmosphere, teachers must constantly rethink their goals, purposes, and definitions. The source of these educational problems extends well beyond the classroom. In cultural critic Raymond Williams' words, "We are talking also, and primarily . . . about an intense crisis of culture and society" (1983, 226).

ESL Literacy as a Social Problem

Americans fear the foreign. In the late twentieth century, xenophobia abounds: a midday talk show host hostilely interrogates a Cuban who operates a successful travel agency. The host wants to know how it is that the Cuban has been able to "make it" here when English is not her native language. On Sunday evening television, an investigative reporter devotes twenty minutes to national worries about the numbers of Asian students gaining admission to America's best universities in spite of their "language problems." And, in California, a physician spearheads an "English Only" campaign which would prohibit or at least restrict the use of "Other" languages.

Apparently, Americans dread multilingualism. Fearing that a polyphony of voices will spoil the nation and lead to chaos, the national consciousness seems to be rehearsing the Tale of Babel. Popular opinion has it that once upon a time America was monolingual and homogeneous. It was a unity which is now fractured by immigrants and their foreign languages. This confabulation implies that monolingualism would restore and preserve American unity, and that governmental legislation impugning all instances of multilingualism would enable a return to this America of lore.

In national consciousness, it is not only legislation but also, and perhaps more importantly, the institutions and the processes of schooling that are responsible for deflecting the chaos of Babel. For academics, even for those who reject caveats against all things foreign, the nonnative speaker of English has become an issue of contention. In the midst of a national "literacy crisis," attention is sharply focused on the writing and reading abilities of these non-native students.

Until recently, the writing of nonnative speakers of English has been largely invisible within American schooling. Now, writers from all over the world are using English. Reed Way Dasenbrock argues that from 1979–1990, the "explosion" of writing by nonnative speak-ers has "come to dominate literature in English today" (1987, 10). This writing, which had been suppressed, ignored, or side-stepped, has become salient, problematic, and provocative. Dasenbrock notes that there "seem to be real barriers to a broad understanding and appreciation of that literature" (1987, 10). Dwight Purdy, a veteran writing program administrator, describes the situation in American universities as follows:

> Today masses of students enter college who could not have entered twenty years ago. Because of them, programs in basic or remedial writing and ESL are everywhere. This significant number of unpre-pared students . . . has forced a shift in expectations throughout our composition programs. (1986, 793)

Purdy's characterization typifies the notice being given to the nonnative speaking student; increasingly, if only in the footnote of a journal article or the subordinate clause of a decanal memo, educators comment on the "increasing number of nonnative speak-ers" that they are "confronted with" in their classes (Pringle 1985, 130). Purdy believes that those "masses" of students have a nega-tive effect on the university, including "the diluting of intellectual expectations" for composition courses (1986, 792). These students are decried as pariahs of the university, the complications of the community college, and masses of unending needs at the adult school.

Purdy's description also exemplifies a pervasive tendency to reduce the nonnative writer to the status of the "unprepared," the disabled one who errs and is "halt and lame" (1986, 795), producing assignments that "do not sound like English," filling out job applica-tions that are "barely literate." In this denunciatory atmosphere, instructors, particularly those who align themselves with the field of teaching English as a Second Language, are pressured to find chimerical methods to eradicate error, to transform nonnative speak-ers into native speakers, and relieve all self-respecting writing and reading programs of their albatross. Purdy hopes that "ESL programs will improve" if and as research focuses on "writing disabilities," and "discovers effective strategies against some forms of endemic error" (1986, 795).

With fears reminiscent of Babel, many academics claim that the writing of the nonnative speaker, polyphonic, heteroglossic, and full of "error," could threaten the very integrity of our educational system. So, schools institute more and "harder" composition courses and more and more exit exams for nonnatives. They justify these requirements in several ways: They need to prepare students for a hypothetical business community that requires nonnative speakers to compose by themselves, rather than collaboratively, quickly and on-the-spot, in "perfect" "standard" English. They need to protect the integrity of a degree from an American university, meaning that nonnative writing somehow compromises these standards. Relatedly, they need to certify the curricula of their liberal arts courses. And, they need to protect students from failure in other disciplines. Ironically, the course these ESL students seem to fail most often is the English department writing course, not chemistry or psychology or philosophy.

Wittingly or not, the literacy/composition course and its instructor have come to function as gatekeepers. This gatekeeping may begin in primary or secondary schools, discouraging many students from ever attempting higher education. Many adult education courses treat literacy as a technical skill, a necessity for employment, or as a luxury unaffordable to those who do not yet speak the language fluently. Even though many of these adult education programs claim to open societal and economic doors, in many, literacy again functions in gatekeeping capacities. Well-meaning teachers find themselves in this role, at least in part, because of the poverty of theory about ESL literacy education.

ESL Literacy as a Theoretical Problem

While literary critics and teachers of ESL, composition, and adult education are clearly vexed by nonnative writers and their texts, it is not solely, or even primarily, a surge in the numbers of students and an "explosion" in the numbers of texts that is the problem. The problem seems rather to stem from a lacuna in theory. Henry Louis Gates, Jr., identifies one source of this gap: The question of the place of texts written by the

> Other (be that odd metaphorical negation of the European defined as African, Arabic, Chinese, Latin American, Yiddish or female authors) in the proper study of "literature," "Western literature," or

"comparative literature" has, until recently, remained an unasked
question, suspended or silenced. . . . (1985, 2)

Writing by the nonnative speaker of English is a manifestation of the
discourse of the Other that the American academy has not been able
to conceptualize adequately.

ESL literacy education needs to dramatically escalate its theoretical self-consciousness. Theories that have been invoked to describe
ESL literacy result in its invisibility, its transformation to speech.
Linguists, for example, have been interested in nonnative speakers
of English, but have considered their writing primarily as a record of
their acquisition of English. Linguistic theory has prevented researchers from perceiving the activity as a whole and inquiring into
its social meaning.

In departments of English, it would seem that poststructuralists—
the pundits of pluralism, the decentered subject, and indeterminacy
—would welcome the discourse of the Other. Yet, when confronted
with the actual accented word and the foreign presence, even self-
acclaimed poststructuralists may express only their concern about
standards and about how soon the foreigner will be able to participate
in the "mainstream." They reinstate the monologic voice, revive the
canon and lobby for texts written in unaccented English. They also
reveal an enormous schism between theory and praxis.

There are dissenting voices. Jay Robinson, of the University
of Michigan, reverses this argument. Robinson contends both that
these students bring a salutary diversity to the academy and that
changes in the student profile parallel the ongoing fertilization of
disciplines that anthropologist Clifford Geertz (1983, 20) has referred
to as "blurred genres." The increasingly varied students, including
large numbers of nonnative speakers, and the increasingly diverse
academy together provide a rationale, if not a mandate, for a reform
of English studies. Robinson sees incipient change as beneficent; he
argues that English studies will benefit rather than suffer by attending to the needs of linguistically "different" students (1985, 489–90).

By making salient the theoretical and social problems of ESL
literacy education and by defining a theoretical framework that can
guide ESL literacy education, I hope to connect praxis and theory. I
use the term literacy "as a kind of shorthand for the social practice
and conceptions of reading and writing" (Street 1984, 1). Literacy is
also the chosen expression because it denotes a broadly based inter-
disciplinary approach to the study of written language. I draw on
theory from the fields of ESL, linguistics, applied linguistics, composition, anthropology, rhetoric, and literary criticism to discuss the
meaning of ESL literacy as a social practice.

My method throughout the book mirrors the thesis. I argue not only that ESL literacy is a social activity but that our understanding of it is socially constructed as well. This means that I look at empirical research as a social artifact, as the product of historically situated discourse. The power of any particular understanding of ESL literacy is less dependent on its empirical validity than on social processes. Rather than attempt to do a broad or narrow empirical study of ESL literacy, I have chosen to "read" and interpret our current understandings of ESL literacy, with the premise that literacy is what we understand it to be. To characterize how ESL literacy is a social practice, I draw on theory and research, on students', literary critics', and published authors' accounts of ESL literacy.

Appropriating Literacy should interest all ESL, literacy, and composition instructors, but its concerns should also touch administrators involved in educating the nonnative speaker of English. My most ambitious aim is to describe a pedagogy of literacy that recognizes and explores the openness of English and allows for the continual formation and transformation of culture and community. My claim is that such a pedagogy will enable readers and writers to revel in, rather than shrink from, the dynamics of identity and difference that form their encounters with ESL readers and writers.

The Chapters: An Overview

In the book as a whole, I wrestle with the question: What does it mean to write and read in a second language? In the first chapter I explore the evolving definitions of literacy in the field of ESL. I look carefully at explicit theorizing about literacy, investigating the assumptions, attitudes, and intellectual climates that have influenced educators and applied linguists. Perhaps the most obvious place to begin is with linguistic theory since it has provided, both directly and indirectly, the intellectual grounds for most of what ESL teachers do in their classes. I survey descriptions of literacy that the field of ESL inherited from structural linguistics. I also examine the cognitive and individualist underpinnings of Chomskian linguistics and similar work in composition, research such as the composing process studies. The chapter is organized somewhat historically. But this must be a ragged history, one with connections more labyrinthine than linear for it is easier to trace the development of ideas within linguistics than it is to adequately discuss why ESL teachers conceive of literacy as they do and how their ideas about literacy are connected to disciplinary paradigms. Perhaps the difficulty of this analysis is to be expected; the route from theory to practice is always circuitous.

While Chapter 1 deals with the *explicit* theories of literacy that ESL inherited from linguistics and composition theory, in Chapter 2, I focus on social meanings of ESL literacy that are *implicit* in theory. I examine how ESL literacy involves cultural, social, and political action. I am specifically interested in the ideologies implicit in the purposes and goals we ascribe to ESL literacy. I examine the statements of ESL authors about their practices and point out that their beliefs about ESL literacy may differ from those on which ESL instructors base their curricula.

In the third chapter I outline a dialectical theory of ESL literacy as a social act. After pointing out the inadequacies of the narrowly psychological, cognitive, and individualist perspectives on ESL literacy, I develop a dialectical framework for ESL literacy through the language theory of M. M. Bakhtin and Lev Vygotsky.

In Chapter 4, Carlos Bulosan's autobiography *America Is in the Heart* provides a clear example of the dialectics described in Chapter 3. Caught in a dialectical whirl, Bulosan continually embraces English literacy only to reject, or at least, resist it soon after. Throughout his life, Bulosan used English literacy to form various community connections and to strive for universalism, a feeling of brotherhood with all.

Chapter 5 elaborates the connections between theory and practice, looking at teaching practices which have been shaped by a social perspective on ESL literacy. The construct of *communitas*, drawn from anthropologist Victor Turner, provides a root metaphor which will help teachers learn how to take advantage of the dialectics of ESL literacy. Included are stories of ESL literacy classes that work, and a list of principles that can generate similar educational practices.

Chapter 6 examines the ways in which teachers construct meaning out of nonnative prose. It looks at the possibilities for negotiation of meaning between the writer, the text, and the teacher. The chapter reports on studies of ESL teachers' reading their student texts and argues that their readings are too narrow. This argument is followed by examples of "reading differently." This latter vocabulary of response is built from Bakhtin's notions of heteroglossia and polyphony.

Notes

1. In this book I do not make any distinction between ESL and EFL, between English studied as an additional language in the United States and outside the United States. I also use the term "the field of ESL" repeatedly. By this I

mean teachers and researchers working with students whose first language is not English.

This book addresses the topic of writing and reading education for adult ESL students at all levels; the term "literacy" is not meant to denote a particular educational level. The term literacy is explained briefly in the introduction and at length in Chapter 3.

Chapter One

A Survey of Linguistic Theory and Concepts of ESL Literacy

What does it mean to write and read in a second language? How do teachers of English as a Second Language (ESL) conceive of literacy? How do they conceive of their role in developing students' English literacy? How have ESL teachers and students arrived at their ideas about literacy? To find answers to these questions, I begin by looking carefully at explicit theorizing about literacy in the field of ESL, investigating the assumptions, attitudes, and intellectual climates that have influenced educators and applied linguists. This survey begins with linguistic theory since it has provided, both directly and indirectly, the intellectual grounds for most of what ESL teachers do in their classes. When ESL scholars and teachers have realized that linguistics could not wholly account for literacy, they have looked to composition and literacy theory to fill in the gaps. I am interested in how ESL specialists have applied and interpreted linguistics, composition, and literacy research to form the theories that guide their educational practices. A subtext of this chapter is a critique of the individualist bias that has shaped models of language, language acquisition, and literacy in the United States.

As ESL student populations have changed, ESL teachers have modified their ideas about literacy. They have picked up and dropped, revised, and reinterpreted ideas from linguistics. They have used parts of theories and woven the parts together to make many wholes. An ESL theorist may, for example, scorn the structuralist's notion that language is an assemblage of habits and language acquisition the formation of these habits. This same theorist may simultaneously cherish the structuralist's phonocentrism—the sense that oral language is "natural" and primary and that literacy a secondary trace. Scholars in ESL may seem theoretical eclectics with a bad case of intellectual amnesia when actually they are responding reasonably to a highly mutable world and exceedingly diverse students.

Linguistics has contributed to the confusion that many ESL teachers feel in the face of literacy education. First, American structural linguistics makes literacy into a conceptual no-man's land because most of the terms of linguistic analysis were developed for speech rather than for the *activities* of writing or reading. In effect, this brand of linguistic theory makes an optical illusion of literacy; as it is being described, it disappears and becomes a type of speech. Second, text linguistics makes literacy into a thing. Text linguists do focus on written language and recognize its legitimacy as an object of analysis. Here, however, language structures are center stage. Literacy is wholly the language structures that make up texts, and not a range of human activities. Third, in the field of ESL, literacy becomes conflated with language acquisition. Reading and writing are important only in so far as they reveal the patterns of an ESL student's acquisition process.

For many years, teachers in the field of ESL relied almost exclusively on linguistics for their conception of literacy; as a result, reading and writing were (and still are in many cases) taught as the shadows of speech and/or as language structure. This approach resulted in much frustration and angst on the part of both teachers and students. In recent years, grappling with perceptions of student failure, ESL teachers and researchers have looked beyond linguistics to augment their ideas about literacy with work from cognitive psychology, social psychology, learning theory, composition, rhetoric, and the list could go on.

American Structuralism and Its Conception of Literacy

The field of ESL has held on to an exceedingly limited conception of literacy which has negatively constrained educational practice.[1] This problem began with the so-called structuralist or descriptivist linguists.

American linguistics, developing alongside continental structural linguistics, initially drew much of its inspiration from Ferdinand de Saussure's University of Geneva lectures, edited for publication as *Cours de Linguistique Generale* (1916). Saussure was interested in describing the synchronic system of structural relations that make up a language, a system which may be referred to as a grammar. Linguists working on these descriptions emphasized the autonomy of their enterprise, its independence from other disciplines. Their descriptive models were not based on principles from disciplines such as psychology and sociology. By definition, linguists were interested in how language was structured, not in how language was related to the social world or the mind.

Isolated from the continental structuralists, American linguistics developed into a separate school with a professedly egalitarian rhetoric. American structuralists were committed to a "value-free" method of language description. They believed that even though languages are diverse in structure, they function equally well in meeting the communicative needs of the people who use them. In fact, according to Frederick J. Newmeyer, this "egalitarian principle" was "the cause around which [the American structuralists] could crystalize their professional identity." This egalitarianism was "even responsible for the decision to found the Linguistic Society of America in 1924" so as to "counteract resistance to the idea that the languages of highly civilized people were on a par with those of savages" (1986, 41).

Much of the ethos of early American linguistics can be traced to Franz Boas who was interested in documenting American Indian languages. Far more than a taxonomist, he continually made the ideological point that human languages are extremely diverse. In the introduction to his 1911 *Handbook of American Indian Languages*, Boas rejected the kind of grammatical analysis that effaced linguistic variation by forcing non-European languages into categories developed to describe European ones. Boas also decried ethnocentric evaluations of non-European languages, repudiating claims that European languages are intrinsically more capable of expressing abstraction than so-called primitive languages.

Boas' interest in the diversity of human languages was maintained in the projects of linguist Leonard Bloomfield and his followers, who gave clear shape and definition to the American school of structural or descriptive linguistics. Bloomfield strongly opposed universalizing trends in thought about language. "Because the Greeks studied only their own language," Bloomfield wrote, they thought it "embodied universal forms of human thought or perhaps the cosmic order," an idea that had been widely and tenaciously accepted for thousands of years (1933, 5).

For the purposes of this discussion, the most important of Bloomfield's ideas is that "writing is *not* language, but merely a way of recording language by means of visible marks" (1933, 21 emphasis added). Bloomfield's disavowal of writing was congruent with his liberal ideology eschewing elitism and ethnocentrism. "All writing ... has remained, almost to our day, the property of only a chosen few," he argued (1933, 13). Reasoning that while all human societies possessed speech, Bloomfield stressed that writing was a relatively recent and elite technology. The philologists, precursors to the structuralists, had privileged writing and Bloomfield considered their ideas scientifically unsound and ideologically repugnant:

> This failure to distinguish between actual speech and the use of writing distorted also their notions about the history of language. . . . They concluded that languages are preserved by the usage of the educated and careful people and changed by the corruptions of the vulgar. In the case of modern languages like English, they believed, accordingly that the speech-forms of books and of upper-class conversation represented an older and purer level, from which the 'vulgarism' of the common people had branched off as 'corruptions' by a process of 'linguistic decay.' (1933, 8)

In line with the principles of autonomous linguistics, Bloomfield believed that a theory of language should be "mechanistic" in two senses: it should be self-contained, its terms and principles referring to no other doctrine than itself, and it should give a physical explanation of language. Speech was reduced to many S-R (stimulus/reaction) series, to movements of the vocal cords and the eardrums. Not surprisingly, language as a whole was nothing more than the sum of many individual "act[s] of speech-utterance." He argued that "the gap between the bodies of the speaker and the hearer—the discontinuity between nervous systems—is bridged by the sound waves" (1933, 26). Speech "mediates" between both the stimulus and the reaction and the speaker and the hearer. As these speech and response sequences become "habits," a child acquires language. Bloomfield opposed "mentalistic" explanations of language in which speech is driven by "some non-physical factor, a spirit or mind (Greek psyche, hence the term psychology) that is present in every human being" (1933, 32).

While many of Bloomfield's ideas became the central principles of American linguistics, his egalitarian agenda was short-circuited in the discipline. According to Dell Hymes, structural linguistics in the 1940s came to possess a "distinct empiricist and xenophobic character" because of the concentration of leading figures developing language teaching materials for the United States military (1981, 16). Another and equally powerful factor in the demise of the liberal tenor of American linguistics was that many of Bloomfield's followers had been contributing members of the Summer Institute of Linguistics (SIL). The SIL's goal was far from the structuralist's stated aim to create a "value-free" science of language. Rather, the SIL aimed to provide "every person . . . [with] a New Testament in his own language," a highly and forthrightly ideological aim (Pike 1977, 11).

As the SIL needed linguists to describe and create writing systems for myriads of "exotic" languages, Bible translation efforts became symbiotically linked to the enterprise of structuralist linguists. As a result, the SIL indirectly helped to form American linguists' attitudes toward the study of literacy. Interests in writing or in texts became associated in their minds with the proselytizing efforts of the SIL: the New Testament was the only text of concern, and the uses and functions of literacy were of interest strictly because they were part of the missionaries' efforts to civilize the savage, to convert the pagan to Christianity. Interestingly, this association of literacy, defined as the printed word itself, with the power to domesticate and civilize is retained in the work of some contemporary literacy theorists such as Walter Ong, S. J.

Linguistic Theory into ESL Education: The Bloomfieldian Legacy

The structuralist linguists claimed that their approach to language lent itself directly to pedagogical application. In 1945 Charles Fries argued that

> the modern scientific study of language has within the last twenty years developed special techniques of descriptive analysis by which a trained linguist can efficiently and accurately arrive at the fundamentally significant matters of structure and sound system amid the bewildering mass of details which constitute the actual rumble of speech. If an adult is to gain a satisfactory proficiency in a foreign language most quickly and easily he must have satisfactory materials on which to work. (5)

Repeatedly, Fries contended that linguists and linguistic analysis were the sole source of these "satisfactory materials." It's hardly surprising that for a Bloomfieldian linguist like Fries, only an "oral approach" would be satisfactory, generating "the basic drill, the repeated repetitions of the patterns produced by a native speaker of the foreign language."

In a classically structuralist statement Fries argues that

> the practice which the student contributes must be oral practice. No matter if the final result desired is to read the foreign language the mastery of the fundamentals of the language—the structure and the sound system with a limited vocabulary—must be through speech.

> *The speech is the language. The written word is but a secondary representation of the language.* (6, emphasis added)

This approach to teaching second languages was derived from and supported by the mechanistic definition of language acquisition and language originally specified by Bloomfield. In his *Outline Guide for the Practical Study of Foreign Languages*, Bloomfield wrote, "the command of a language is not a matter of knowledge; the speakers are quite unable to describe the habits which make up their language. The command of a language is a matter of practice" (1942, 12). This "oral approach," sometimes referred to as the "audiolingual method," presumes that literacy practices are wholly dependent on the development processes of oral language. And for many years, no respectable applied linguist would have doubted that

> before the students can [read for comprehension] very well, the connection between the sound and its written symbol (or symbols) needs to be firmly established. The importance of this relationship must not be underestimated, and sufficient practice to establish this sound-symbol relationship should be provided. (Chastain 1976, 309)

In the late twentieth century, some psycholinguists and reading specialists may challenge this idea, but many ESL practitioners hold steadfastly to their Bloomfieldian belief in the ironclad union of sound and symbol in teaching reading.

The influence of these linguists/language educators lasted well beyond the postwar years. In 1964, Robert Lado published a not atypical book entitled *Second Language Teaching: A Scientific Approach*. In this handbook, he defines learning to write as "learning to put down at a speed greater than that of drawing, the conventional symbols of the writing system, symbols that represent the utterances one has in mind" (59). Lado also suggests that students can learn to write in a second language by "corresponding," but he adds the caveat that for this method to prove effective, the correspondent must correct the letters and send them back (1964, 92). This picture of literacy processes is highly mechanistic, particularly in its emphasis on the one-to-one correspondence between the utterance (in mind) and writing and the relation of speed to writing.

Lado's ideas about literacy, in keeping with contemporary linguistics, were the logical result of Bloomfield's and later Watson and Skinner's stimulus-response theory of language acquisition. Lado and his contemporaries drew both their notion of the scientific approach and their definition of the writing process from the "science" of descriptive linguistics developed by the structuralists. In research and pedagogy, Lado et al. maintained that writing processes differed only incidentally from those of speech; writing was understood to be very simply the inscription of the "speech utterances one has in mind."

Lado's views were not anomalous. For many early American linguists, literacy was irrelevant, a type of speech, a shadow of speech, and/or a record of speech. Naturally when ESL specialists applied Bloomfieldian precepts, they imported his ideas about literacy. As a result, writing in the ESL classroom came to consist of exercises in which students practiced inscribing correct language forms, or "structures." There was great emphasis on protecting the student from making errors in their writing. The primary technique was called "controlled composition." Typical of the rationale for controlled composition is this 1964 edict to ESL teachers: "Free composition is in direct opposition to the expressed ideas of habit-forming teaching methods which strive to prevent error from occurring" (Pincus 1964, 186). Because of the Bloomfieldian influence, in the field of ESL, literacy has often been conflated with language acquisition, and writing has been represented as "the mastery of sentence patterns . . . , the formation of a habit" (Zamel 1976, 70).

Since the late 1970s, ESL specialists have questioned the idea of language as habit and language acquisition as habit formation, and they have also relinquished some of their concern over controlling students' written language. Still, literacy is often viewed as language practice; students write and read to practice English. This practice is organized around texts which are strikingly artificial, disembodied of any authorial purpose or intention. They are not short stories or letters or grocery lists. They are contextless sentences or paragraphs like this one entitled "Miriam's Routine" : "Miriam cooks breakfast every morning. After breakfast she washes the dishes and cleans the house. She listens to the radio as she works" (Byrd 1991, 55). The passage was designed to provide the student with practice on the present tense. Following the text are student exercises which consist of true/false comprehension questions, rewriting the paragraph with the past tense and with the plural subject "Miriam and Joanne." Students finish the unit by writing on lines provided in the book itself about their "daily routine on the days [they] go to school or work." Literacy construed as practice for language acquisition is phony and constrained.

In adult school education, at least some ESL teachers have continued to subscribe to the Bloomfieldian ideology as it was translated into pedagogical practice by Charles Fries in the 1940s. They have viewed literacy as an elitist practice. In the name of learner centered education, they may focus on "oral fluency" and "survival skills." Unfortunately the Friesian legacy can prevent teachers from seeing the ways in which literacy and orality are interdependent in every-day life. For example, in a 1987 documentary that emphasized the cultural conflicts, confusion, and hardships faced by Hmong refugees in California, teachers in an adult school program stated that "in our classes the emphasis is on speaking comprehension. *Writing is secondary*" (emphasis added). Ironically this statement was juxta-posed with those of social workers who described the Hmong's pri-mary problems as resulting from "an inability to move through social systems that require so much writing and reading" (*The Hmong: Our Newest Neighbors*).

The description of these classes is indicative of the tenacity of the Bloomfieldian view of literacy in ESL as a whole. While ESL teachers exclaim that "further research and training are sorely needed in ESL literacy" (Epstein 1985, 8), their concern has generally been restricted to selecting methods. The lack of debate over what literacy is and how it develops serves as further evidence of the Bloomfieldian hegemony. Instruction, it is believed, should follow the "*natural* pattern of language acquisition: listening, speaking, reading and writing." It follows then that "In ESL literacy, the learner should read and write only the language he or she comprehends [orally]" (Bright, qtd in Epstein 1985, 5, emphasis added). Ulti-mately, literacy is understood as a code that functions as a conduit for the writer's speechlike utterance.

Edward Sapir, Benjamin Whorf: Culture and Language

The shape of American structural linguistics was also influenced by the projects of Edward Sapir, a linguist less intent on scientific pos-turing than Bloomfield and his cohorts. Sapir was intrigued by the relationship of culture to language. Sapir believed that the structure of one's language directly shapes one's view of the world and that linguistic structures shape one's perception of reality:

> Language . . . actually defines experience for us by reason of its formal completeness and because of our unconscious projection of its implicit expectations into the field of experience. . . . Such cate-gories as number, gender, case and tense . . . are as much discovered in experience as imposed upon it because of the tyrannical hold that linguistic form has upon our orientation in the world. (1931, 578)

This doctrine, elaborated in large part by Benjamin Whorf, has been called the Sapir-Whorf hypothesis and has proven to be the most powerful of American attempts to forge a linkage between language structure and social phenomena such as culture.

Sapir's work differed in scope, method, and general tenor from that of Bloomfield. Although Sapir shared Bloomfield's opposition to linguistic analysis that privileged writing over speech, Sapir continued to find writing a legitimate object of analysis. A token of this conviction can be found in his "Language and Literature" chapter in the book *Language*. In stark contrast, Bloomfield proclaimed, in his own manifesto entitled *Language*: "A student of writing, of literature or philology might realize, after some *waste* of effort, that he had better first study language and then return to these problems" (1933, 22, emphasis added). In other words, for Bloomfield, literacy was not a pertinent theoretical problem because writing was not language. Furthermore, while Bloomfield explained language in strictly organic or physical terms, Sapir argued that language is "a cultural, not a biologically inherited, function" (1921, vii).

Perhaps, however, their fundamental difference was one of method; Sapir openly resisted the empiricist trend in American descriptive linguistics, and Bloomfield responded by calling Sapir a "medicine man" (Jakobson 1979, 107). Although the Sapir-Whorf hypothesis provided linguist/language educators with a theoretical alternative to Bloomfieldian behaviorism, Sapir's ideas were not widely applied in ESL because they were not viewed as compatible with a systematic "scientific" approach to language. To ESL professionals raised on Lado and Fries, Sapir's ideas appeared as so much tautological, unverifiable mumbo jumbo.

ESL Literacy and Contrastive Rhetoric

Nevertheless, the field of ESL incorporated some of Sapir's ideas about the connection between language and culture via Robert B. Kaplan's project of contrastive rhetoric. As a linguist and ESL specialist, Kaplan has been concerned with composition instruction for foreign students. The question that seemed to motivate his project originally, in the late 1960s, was why foreign students who "*can* write an adequate essay in their native language *cannot* write an adequate essay in a second language" ([1966] 1972, 247, emphasis added).

Kaplan began to address this problem in an article entitled "Cultural Thought Patterns in Inter-cultural Education" ([1966] 1972). Outlining the enterprise of contrastive rhetoric, this article argued that "certain linguistic structures are best comprehended as embodiments of logical structures" ([1966] 1972, 247), an idea clearly aligned with the Sapir-Whorf hypothesis. Quoting from Leo Spitzer, Kaplan maintained:

> every language offers to its speakers a ready-made interpretation of
> the world, truly a Weltanschauung, a metaphysical word-picture
> which, after having originated in the thinking of our ancestors,
> tends to impose itself ever anew on posterity. Take for instance a
> simple sentence such as 'I see him. . . .' this means that English, and
> I might say, Indo-European, presents the impressions made on our
> senses predominantly as human activities, brought about by our
> will. But the Eskimos in Greenland say not 'I see him' but 'he
> appears to me . . .' Thus the Indo-European speaker conceives as
> workings of his activities what the fatalistic Eskimo sees as events
> that happen to him. ([1966] 1972, 246–7)

Kaplan, drawing on Michael Polyani and Leo Spizer, seems particularly remote from Bloomfield when he equates writing with rhetoric
and rhetoric in turn, with logic ([1966] 1972, 247):

> Rhetorical logic (as distinct from mathematical logic) is shaped
> by the culture in which it has developed and circularly, it meets
> the approval of the society which shapes it. The approval of a
> society is expressed through preferences for certain kinds of dis-
> course patterns, and implicitly through the rejection of other organi-
> zational patterns which do not conform to the approved conventions.
> (1972, 20)

Kaplan continued by providing examples of "discourse patterns."
"Arabic," he claims, "is dominated by an elaborate parallel structure,
a repetition of sound, of syntax and of thought" ([1966] 1972, 248).
Kaplan also maintained that these textual conventions or discourse
patterns are socially established and maintained. Ontogenetically,
they are historical and cultural rather than biologically "natural" or
universal. In later discussions, Kaplan has stressed that writing is
"post-biological." Kaplan elaborates this idea by arguing that all of
the "rhetorical modes" are possible in any language. "The issue is
that each language has certain clear preferences, so that while all
forms are possible, all forms do not occur with equal frequency"
(1987, 10).

Early contrastive rhetoric relied heavily on the methods and pre-
dictive powers of contrastive analysis, which in its strongest form
would say that the errors ESL learners make result from the structures of their first languages; the first language *interferes* with the
second language. The elements of the second language that are similar to the learner's native language are supposedly simple for learners
and those areas that are different are difficult (Lado 1957, 2, emphasis
added).

The pedagogical problem for nonnative writers was also called
"interference" by Kaplan and his colleagues. Kaplan argued that the
thought sequences from the students' native languages would

"interfere" with their writing in English. The texts of nonnative speakers were "foreign sounding" because they violated the expected "logic" or sequences of thought of native readers. ([1966] 1972, 247). In 1966 Kaplan concluded that the "nonnative speaker learning English" must "master the rhetoric of the English paragraph" ([1966] 1972, 261), implying that this writer will learn in the process to produce English "thought sequences."

In the article which inaugurated contrastive rhetoric, the activity of writing was described as the workings of individual minds, even though Kaplan recognized that social processes are involved in conventionalizing the thought of the individual. Kaplan also argued that texts represent mind in a direct or transparent fashion. Quoting from rhetorician Hans Guth, Kaplan contended that the paragraph is a "logical, rather than a typographical unit" ([1966] 1972, 257–8).

In the ESL community, Kaplan's work has had enormous appeal; for many years his project provided the sole alternative to the Bloomfieldian notion that writing is merely the record of a speech habit. Contrastive rhetoric has given teachers a vocabulary to talk about more than "Classroom Techniques for Controlling Composition" (Slager 1966, 224–45). Unfortunately, however, Kaplan's structuralist bias has restricted his interest in literacy to the text and its internal relations. Although Kaplan has recognized the influence of culture on language, the terms of his methodology seem to prevent him from advancing beyond the understanding that culture is statically embedded in language. Contrastive rhetoric has lacked a dialectic of language and culture, an understanding that the language and culture are dynamically and symbiotically involved in shaping one another.

Much of the recent work in contrastive rhetoric questions or at least circumvents this explicit and narrow equation of rhetoric and thought. Carolyn Matalene, for example, rejects Kaplan's equation of logic and rhetoric. She reappropriates at least part of the understanding of rhetoric codified in the Western rhetorical tradition by revising the "rhetoric" of "contrastive rhetoric" to "a way of thinking about the relationships that exist among speaker, subject matter, purpose and audience" (1985, 789). Matalene recognizes her own departure from the structuralist tradition that informs Kaplan's earliest versions of "contrastive rhetoric." She criticizes the bias of ESL researchers who "take a structuralist approach and focus on rhetoric as organization; they do not discuss the larger contexts—psychological, social or cultural—which also constitute rhetoric" (1985, 847). For Matalene contrastive rhetoric becomes an analysis of the ways in which texts mediate social relationships. Her understanding enables her to make the following statement:

> For the Chinese, then, the primary function of rhetoric is to preserve
> the general harmony and to promote social cohesion; . . . its tech-
> nique always the repetition of maxims, exempla and analogies pre-
> sented in established forms and expressed in well-known phrases.
> (1985, 795)

In a similar vein, John Hinds contrasts the written rhetoric of
Japan and the United States. What he is really juxtaposing are
reader/listener expectations about explicitness of information: "I
take as a starting point the position that English speakers, by and
large, charge the writer, or speaker, with the responsibility to make
clear and well-organized statements" (1987, 43). Hinds contends
that the opposite is true of the Japanese. Even Hinds, however, ends
a perceptive article with the structuralist sleight of hand. Finally, he
locates these expectations in the structures of the language of the
text, even at the sentence level. Shirley Ostler also uses a mix of
structuralist, historical, and rhetorical modes of explanation. In
examining the problems Arabic students have in writing for the
American university, she begins "Specifically, the hypothesis of
this paper is that the rhetoric of Classical Arabic is closely tied to
the *system* of that language" (1987, 73, emphasis added). Interestingly, Ostler connects the syntax of Arabic to the social and cultural
history of Arabic literacy. She argues, for example, that "the illiterate
peasants prefer the highly literate, Classical Arabic which they perhaps only partially understand, to the vernacular in which they
are fluent. As was true in the England of John Lyly, the beauty of
form is valued more highly than content." This sentiment, Ostler
suggests, arises from the symbiotic relationship between all Arabic
literacy and the Qu'ran and "the very structure of [its] language"
(1987, 73).

While accepting its general premises, many critics of contrastive
rhetoric balk at its pedagogical agenda. Yoshitaro Nishimura declares
that his own work "does not report a description of the deviation
from the native and standard English but it will rather declare a
positive independence for which we demand tolerance from the
natives" (1979, 8). Accordingly, Nishimura arrives at the following
pedagogical conclusion:

> If we correct Japanese student . . . so that we may accomplish West-
> ern rule, we thoroughly suppress their motivation to create ideas
> into composition. It is of no importance whether Western type of
> paragraph structure can be teachable to adult learners or not. It is
> of the biggest significance whether Western or English block-style of
> logic, and Eastern, or Japanese flowing-style of thought, East and
> West should be tolerant of each other. (1979, 9)

Nishimura's views are hardly idiosyncratic; a growing number of analysts welcome the "new types of essays" developed by nonnative speakers of English (Harder 1980, 23). Caroline Matalene finds it exciting that "[teachers] can witness and perhaps even inspire the extraordinary syntheses that are possible when a brilliant student integrates Eastern and Western rhetoric" (1985, 804).

For over twenty years Kaplan has insisted that "written language discourse deserves study separate from oral discourse" (1987,18). "In the end the study of written text as a distinct linguistic phenomenon governed by a set of rules at least partially different from the sets which apply to other linguistic phenomena is legitimate. . . ." Yet, in focusing on text structure and rhetorical organization, he continues to ask the wrong questions:

> If, for example, one wishes to produce texts to be read by village women in sectors of Southeast Asia, what *organization of text* is most likely to introduce that audience to basic child nutrition in the most effective manner, and how will that *rhetorical structure* differ from one intended to serve the same purposes for women in sectors of the Arab Middle East? (1987, 20, emphasis added)

In the project of contrastive rhetoric, rhetoric itself is reduced to structure and literacy distilled to thought.

Chomsky and the Reintroduction of Mind

Theorists conceive of ESL writing in accordance with their ideas about (second) language acquisition, their concept of literacy, and, perhaps most importantly, their notion of the relationship between language acquisition and literacy. As linguistics took a turn and began to focus on the mind and posit its natural, individual relation to language and language acquisition, the field of ESL began to connect literacy with thought as well as with speech. In contrastive rhetoric, for example, the emphasis on thought and mind probably came as much from the influence of Noam Chomsky as from Sapir. Indirectly, Noam Chomsky and his challenge to Bloomfieldian linguistics reopened the question of ESL literacy for those in the field of ESL.

Beginning in 1957, with the publication of *Syntactic Structures*, Noam Chomsky changed the direction of American linguistics. Chomsky questioned the empiricist concept of science held by the American structuralists (Newmeyer 1986, 66), maintaining that nothing was to be gained from the empiricist program to obtain "objectivity." In Chomsky's view, what the Bloomfieldians actually proved was that "objectivity can be pursued with little consequence gained in insight and understanding" (1965, 20). In reaction to the empiricist and mechanistic bent of the American structuralists, Chomsky revived and refined the "mentalist" conception of language popular from the seventeenth to the mid-nineteenth century. He used this new mentalism to explain language acquisition and the nature of language structure. The notions of "innate ideas" and "mind" were of particular interest to him, not just as rhetorical topics with which to refute Bloomfield's mechanism, but as the grounds for understanding certain "language universals": Chomsky argued that "the general features of grammatical structure are common to all languages and reflect certain fundamental properties of the human mind" (1966, 59).

Many of Chomsky's ideas were inspired by Wilhelm von Humboldt (1833). On the first pages of *Aspects*, Chomsky credited Von Humboldt with the idea that "a language is based on a system of rules determining the interpretation of its infinitely many sentences," the informing principle for generative grammar (1965, v). In this text, Chomsky's view of language acquisition is also basically Humboldtian: a perspective in which language is viewed as "unlearned behavior which somehow develops from within in an essentially predetermined way" (1966). This mentalist or rationalist position assumes a special inborn capacity for language, a set of psychological predispositions which are specifically linguistic. In Chomsky's model this "innate equipment that a child brings to bear in language learning" (1962, 530) is referred to as the language-acquisition device, or LAD. Chomsky's LAD, however, is not understood to be a dynamic process or set of procedures. In fact, psycholinguist Daniel Slobin has labeled Chomsky's formulation as a "content view" of language acquisition (1966, 88) because the LAD is associated not with processes but with innate structures of mind; it is a "mental organ" constrained by an innate and universal grammar (Chomsky 1980).

Employing these mentalist presuppositions, Chomsky distinguished between linguistic knowledge, which he called competence, and use, which he referred to as performance. Following Ferdinand de Saussure, Chomsky did not study the individual concrete speech act or performance. As a result, most linguists after Chomsky privileged the investigation of competence, many ignoring the study of performance altogether. Since its inauguration, Chomsky's competence/performance pair has become so widely absorbed that even when it is repudiated, the distinction defines the rebellion.

Nonetheless, competence is a vague notion. At one time or another Chomsky seems to have advocated at least the three following interpretations: "competence as an idealized model of linguistic performance, competence as a central component of an idealized performance model and competence as an independent, abstract, entity remote from linguistic performance" (Derwing 1973, 259). Competence is related to the idea and use of native-speaker intuition. Intuition accounts for why native speakers can point out agrammatical, equivalent, and ambiguous sentences. This intuition is possible because of competence. The grammar accounts for intuitions. The notion of competence is important because it has been the point of departure for many theories of language acquisition. Indeed, to Chomsky, the study of competence and the study of language acquisition have been equivalent.

ESL Literacy as Thinking and Composing

Chomskian theory has indirectly influenced how the field of ESL has represented the meaning of literacy to itself. The terms through which writing and reading are defined limit how educators perceive and define literacy. Post-Chomskian literacy is valued as evidence of competence or knowledge of linguistic rules. Once again, literacy is conflated with language acquisition. Because Chomskian theory doesn't account for either the ontology of literacy or the relation of writing to speech, ESL teachers and researchers may still define writing as a representation of speech, even though they may reject the Bloomfieldian notion that speech is a set of habits.

As Chomsky undercut the power of Bloomfield's mechanistic ideas about language acquisition, ESL specialists became interested in cognitive psychology and its "mentalist," rationalist theory that "learning in general and language learning in particular are internal, mental operations controlled by the individual" (Chastain 1976,146). This characterization of language acquisition was closely related to and in some respects derived from many of Chomsky's notions about the nature of language. And these ideas were easily appropriated by ESL specialists who viewed themselves as applied linguists and found their theoretical bearings in current linguistic models.

The cognitive climate of the 1960s was also a postcolonial era in which English was rapidly becoming a language of world literacy. As more and more students needed to become literate in English, more and more ESL teachers were forced to think seriously about what it means to teach someone to read and write in a second language. The structuralist picture of "writing [as] a secondary representation of the language" (Fries 1945, 6) was not an adequate framework for those educators who looked to it as a guide for their classroom practices.

Chomskian linguistics was of little direct help, and ESL teachers began to look beyond linguistics for definitions of literacy.

The disciplines of English and English education had begun to define writing as composing and composing as a type of thinking. They had begun to investigate the ways in which people write and the ways in which thinking is connected to and defined by the act of writing. ESL specialists felt at home with the composing process studies' image of literacy as an act of individual cognition. In Chomskian linguistics, language was the product of an individual mind, and because literacy was language, it was also the property of an individual. Through its theoretical compatibility with current linguistic theory, composing process studies were extremely attractive to ESL specialists.

In one of the earliest composing studies, Janet Emig analyzed the composing processes of twelfth graders. She looked at composing as a creative process. Adapting the terminology of scholars such as Jerome Bruner, she found "elements, moments, stages within the composing process which can be distinguished and characterized in some detail" (1971, 33). Emig's was merely the first of many studies of the "composing process." Perhaps the best known studies of this sort are the protocol analyses of Linda Flower and cognitive psychologist John Hayes. They asked subjects to talk aloud while they composed. The researchers then transcribed this talk and took it to be evidence of the composing process. Their work has been criticized for its "conflation of discourse and reality" which allowed them to use protocol data "as descriptions of writers' cognitive processes" (Cooper and Holzman [1983] 1989, 75).

In the 1970s some ESL scholars were more influenced by cognitive learning theory and psychology than they were by the work coming out of English departments. Through the cognitive lens, they began to see writing as evidence of thinking. Again, this perspective on writing was not part of the Chomskian model, but the theory did nothing to contradict it. In the early 1970s, Mary Lawrence of the University of Michigan wrote a composition textbook, *Writing as a Thinking Process*, which she based on "the general theoretical principles of cognition . . . [as described by] Jerome S. Bruner of the Center for Cognitive Studies, Harvard University" (1972, 3). She described her approach as "the cognitive method [which] treats writing not as an end-product to be evaluated and graded but as an activity, a process, which the student can learn how to accomplish" (1972, 3).

In the 1970s and early 1980s, composing process research was not a uniform or monolithic project. Many researchers took composing to be the object of analysis yet they asked different questions about the activity. Some valorized the process itself without reference to the quality of the final product. They asked: what is composing? what happens in composing? Among ESL specialists, some early articles of Barry Taylor and Vivian Zamel represent this emphasis.

In their early work, these researchers no longer conflated the processes of language acquisition and the practices of literacy. They dichotomized them. Relying heavily on the terminology of Donald Murray, Barry Taylor, for example, talked of composing as a cognitive process. Composing was only partially linguistic, valued mostly for benefits in cognitive growth and the occasions it brought for "creative discovery" (1981, 6). Taylor, however, also encouraged "developing personal intuitions about what good writing looks like" (1981,12), implying through the Chomskian term *intuition* that he believed in an analogue of linguistic competence pertaining to writing. The processes of language acquisition were separate from those of composing. He suggested that it would be a mistake to value composing for its benefits in terms of second language acquisition, although he equivocated, "it is possible that [language acquisition could occur through] experience in communicating in writing" (1981, 8).

Taylor was not alone in his separation of second-language acquisition and composing. In 1976 Vivian Zamel represented the acquisition of language as chronologically prior to composing (68–9). In her view, one needed to have learned the language before one could compose. Composing, defined as "creating thoughts," is possible only after "students . . . have a basic linguistic competence" (1976, 68). Bloomfield would certainly have found little to quarrel with in the statement that "writing is a culmination of other language skills and . . . composition is therefore dependent on the mastery of listening, speaking and reading" (1976, 68). But by 1982, Zamel had completely separated the language acquisition and composing processes. One composed without engaging in language acquisition. She wrote that "engaging students in the process of composing [does not] eliminate our obligation to upgrade their linguistic *competencies*" (207, emphasis added).

It appears that language acquisition/composing were viewed as discrete processes because process and product were rigidly segregated in some composition studies. As stated above, some theorists paid nearly microscopic attention to the composing process itself and ignored the text that is produced. If teachers showed an interest in the students' final product, they were said to be stifling students' composing processes. These researchers also associated the study of language acquisition with an interest in the accuracy and the error of the final product.

In a 1985 article, ESL researcher Ann Raimes argued that literacy for the nonnative speaker is an opportunity for both language acquisition and idea creation, challenging the logical and chronological separation of language acquisition and composing (as thinking). In her study, she contended that "students at any level of proficiency can be engaged in discovery of meaning" (1985, 250). Further, she maintained that

> Think-aloud composing and analysis of students' language activities while writing have shown the value of writing as a language learning tool. Instead of serving merely as an adjunct to language learning, useful mainly for practice exercises and reinforcement of academic tasks, writing itself has primary value as a language teaching tool. (1985, 252)

Interestingly, the quotation above indicates that even in 1985, Raimes supposed it necessary to argue against Bloomfieldian definitions of literacy and language acquisition. While Chomskian linguistics and composing-process theory had allowed ESL specialists to conceive of writing as a "thinking process," their understanding of ESL writing continued to be a melange of Bloomfieldian and composing-process perspectives.

ESL Literacy as Thinking and Competence

Of those ESL theorists dealing with the second-language writer, Stephen Krashen has most directly employed the Chomskian distinction of competence and performance. Other researchers, even those who accept without hesitation Chomsky's framework which includes "the case that adult native speakers of a language have a competence," have questioned "the validity of an equivalent distinction for the written mode" (Kroll 1978, 176). Krashen, however, assumes that there is definitely such a thing as "writing competence" and that this competence is "the abstract knowledge the proficient writer has about writing" (1984, 20). This abstract knowledge seems to be primarily "knowledge of the code" (1984, 27). Krashen argues that competence is "tacit knowledge of conventions or formal features of reader-based prose" (1984, 20). Quoting from Linda Flower and John Hayes, Krashen adds that competence may include "a set of images of what a text can look like" (1984, 28). Perhaps Krashen does think that competence entails more than knowledge of the code, for he argues that "much of what good writers *do* routinely and subconsciously remains to be discovered" (1984, 25, emphasis added). Or perhaps, he simply thinks that there is more of the code to be discovered.

In general, Krashen "suggests that competence in writing develops the same way competence in second language develops" (1984, 21). To understand this rather extreme statement, one needs to recognize that Krashen conflates the two processes. Writing is language. To learn to write is to acquire the language. As we have seen, in ESL, literacy is conflated with language acquisition over and over again because language acquisition is what ESL scholars theorize about. Krashen is less interested in the composing process in general than in how *good* writing is produced, and the interest he does take in process is subordinated to the product; the process is defined in terms of what a good product would look like. Good writing is good language acquisition.

For Krashen competence or mastery of the code is acquired rather than learned. Language acquisition (as opposed to language learning) is characterized as "a subconscious process similar to child first language acquisition." Acquisition happens when we understand messages in the second language, when we understand what is said or written rather than how it is expressed, when we focus on meaning and not form" (1982, 21). Krashen believes that writers acquire competence through the process of reading for pleasure rather than through writing itself, although he clearly ascribes other "cognitive" benefits to the act of writing. He claims, for example, that "[writing] can make you smarter" (1986, 115). It should be pointed out that it is Chomsky's emphasis on language as "cognition" as opposed to behavior that has allowed linguists such as Krashen (and Kaplan, as discussed above) to conceive of writing as *thinking* rather than as a record of speech.

Literacy as Competence: A Critique

While Chomskian theory has provided a foundation for ESL specialists' theoretical speculation, it has also negatively constrained their concepts of literacy. The competence/performance distinction promotes the notion that language acquisition is a more or less biological and passive process that is ultimately controlled by a language acquisition device. While the LAD is a serious hypothesis which suggests that we are, in a sense, wired for language, the details of the LAD have not been worked out. As a result, to many in ESL pedagogy, the LAD has become a kind of black box that vaguely, but finally, accounts for the processes of language acquisition. From this perspective, the language an ESL writer acquires is reified, and the language acquisition process is somehow logically and even chronologically prior to actual language actions such as literacy practices.

This problem does not result from the model's application to literacy *per se*, but rather from its basic construction; as Chomsky himself has repeatedly insisted, the model's basic terms do not correspond to real-world phenomena. Chomskian theory describes linguistic competence through formalized rules, rules which are designed for formal elegance and internal coherence. These rules are not, in other words, isomorphic with psychological or physiological processes:

> There is what might be called an inferential gap between linguistic formalisms and observable events; indeed, the logical apparatus necessary to bridge the gap is not part of the theoretical structure as such. (Harris 1970, 7)

The interrelationship between competence and performance, how a speaker utilizes his knowledge to perform, remains unarticulated. This may not be a mistake on Chomsky's part, a theoretical oversight, as much as a matter of theoretical necessity:

> There is logical incompatibility between the real-world entity (performance) and its idealized counterpart (competence). Indeed if competence and performance differ in their essential make-up or logical character (as Chomsky suggests, rightly) how are the two to be found compatible within one theory; in particular, how is it possible to construct a P-model which incorporates a generative grammar (C-model) as an essential component? (Derwing 1973, 294)

The Chomskian framework cannot specify, either logically or empirically, the relationship of linguistic knowledge to the act of writing, or to literacy in general. A competence model cannot adequately represent language performance, even idealized performance. Those theorists who accept the Chomskian model but seek to expand it are entrapped by these limitations. The competence/performance distinction, as used by ESL specialists carries with it ungainly theoretical and ideological baggage, much of it unproductive, if not subtly pernicious, to the study of literacy itself. Subscribers to the Chomskian paradigm associate language acquisition with the domain of competence, and the act of composing with performance. Because Chomsky's theory never clearly specifies the relationship between competence and performance, ESL theorists who have relied, albeit indirectly, on his model cannot use it to specify the relationship between second language acquisition and composing.

In trying to establish a "socially constituted linguistics," Dell Hymes, an American sociolinguist, retains and extends the Chomskian competence/performance distinction (1974, 205). Hymes argues that "[Chomsky's] Cartesian linguistics reduces 'competence' to knowledge of grammar, 'performance' to behavior, and 'creativity' to novelty." He further recognizes that "those concerned with linguistic aspects of education and with sociolinguistic theory . . . must reconstruct the concepts for themselves" (1974, 121). He tries to expand the notion of competence beyond the code; "competence [is] personal ability (not just grammatical knowledge, systematic potential of a grammar, superorganic property of a society, or, indeed, irrelevant to persons in any other way)." Performance, in turn, is more than "psycholinguistic processing and impediment" (1974, 206). Hymes' competence and performance are far removed from those of Chomsky, so far that one wonders why he chose to retain the terminology at all.

Chomsky's influence is also retained in the paucity of comparative work, in tacit assumptions about the universality of the composing process. In large part, ESL researchers have assumed that the constructs that are used to describe the composing processes of native-speaking Americans are equally applicable to subjects from very different cultures and social backgrounds.

Social "Factors" and "Aspects" of Language: A Critique

The discipline of linguistics understands language, literacy, and language acquisition to be essentially asocial. Even though premier sociolinguist William Labov would argue that "Language is a form of social behavior" (1972, 183), what he actually studies is "language in its social context" and "the social setting of linguistic change" rather than language as social process (1972, vii). Labov writes as if language were fundamentally individual even though it is acted upon or influenced by such processes as social stratification. Labov is not alone. This tendency occurs throughout *socio* linguistics so much so that researchers Smith, Giles, and Hewstone argue that "There is an implicit dichotomization of language and society to be found almost without exception in sociolinguistics" (Smith, Giles and Hewstone 1980, 284).

American linguistic theory describes language, in its genesis and essence, as constituted by cognitive processes. Social and linguistic development are independent of one another. Sociolinguistic models diverge from a cognitivist paradigm only in that they "factor in social variables to linguistic formulae" (Smith, Giles and Hewstone 1980, 285). ESL research borrows from sociolinguistics to conceive of the social aspects of second language acquisition as "variables" or "factors" which affect but stand outside of the central process of second language acquisition itself. Krashen, for example, does not describe the social interactions in which learners use the second language; instead he talks about a filter which allows or prevents input from reaching the LAD. Krashen's "filter" is not a social process but a mental attitude or state of mind such as ethnocentricity or relaxation.

Krashen's model is familiar in its basic construction. As we have seen, American models of language acquisition are highly psychological; in fact, language acquisition is studied as *psycho*linguistics. Along with psychologists, psycholinguists

> view culture or society as a variable to be incorporated into models of individual functioning. This represents a kind of reductionism which assumes that sociocultural phenomena can ultimately be explained on the basis of psychological processes. (Wertsch 1985, 1)

John Schumann's model of language acquisition has been vulnerable to this "reductionism." Schumann argues that "factors" such as "cultural congruity, desire to assimilate, degree of social equality" determine in some objective fashion the amount of social distance between second language and [English speaking] groups. He predicts that a large amount of social distance inhibits second language acquisition while little distance enhances the process. Social distance, however, is not a social process. At least, the details of the social processes entailed in social distance are not developed. As a result, ESL researchers psychologize the concept and the model itself so that they can work with it:

> But it is unclear how these variables are to be measured (Brown 1980), and, in any event, it is not objective conditions but what the learner perceives that forms the learner's reality (Acton 1979). This reality is constantly shifting as the individual's perceptions change. In this sense *considerations of social distance reduce to questions of psychological distance.* (McLaughlin 1987, 126, emphasis added)

While some other second language acquisition researchers appear to focus on the processes of second language acquisition, describing learners' active creation of hypotheses (Dulay and Burt 1974, 95–123) about the "target language," their approximative systems (Nemser [1971] 1974, 55–63) or their "interlanguage" (Selinker 1974, 31–54), what these researchers actually describe are language structures rather than social interactions which bring about language structures.[2]

Having mounted a critique of sociolinguistics, social psychologists may credit themselves with possessing an antidote to the miasma of cognitive theories of language. Social psychologists, however, do not radically depart from the sociolinguistic approach to language which they censure; while social psychology describes itself as the study of interaction, its primary object of analysis may remain the cognitive processes of the individual. In social psychologists' own terms, "[the field] emphasizes the cognitive processes that mediate between social stimuli and overt behavior." And further, in much social psychological research, the social is reduced to a stimulus that "contributes to the individual's cognitive organization" (Smith, Giles and Hewstone 1980, 288). Whereas sociolinguistics introduces social factors into an explanation of language, social psychologists factor both language and social interaction into formulae for cognitive processes. While the object of analysis is somewhat different for sociolinguistics and social psychology, the fields construe the relationship of language to social interaction similarly, with social interaction remaining peripheral in both models.

Even social psychologists Robert Gardner and Wallace Lambert psychologize social processes as they try to answer the question: "How is it that some people can learn a foreign language quickly and expertly while others, given the same opportunities to learn, are utter failures?" (1972, 1). The conclusion they have drawn is that "mastering a foreign language depends on the willingness and orientation to be like representative members of the language community and to become associated at least vicariously with that other community" (1972, 14). For Gardner and Lambert, the social is a constellation of "factors" creating "motivation," which is essentially a psychological state—"a willingness and orientation," to use their own terms. They do not examine or specify the characteristics of the actual interactions and associations between native and nonnative speakers.

Just as the social processes of language acquisition remain hidden in ESL, so the social processes that constitute second language literacy remain largely unexamined. Accordingly, it is predictable that ESL scholars who investigate literacy may define the object of their analysis as the *mental processes* of the learner/writer," the "*psycholinguistic* reality of the *human mind* beyond the page" (Kroll 1978, 179 emphasis added).

Essayist Literacy—Full Circle from Bloomfield

Several ESL specialists have turned their attention to the work of David Olson, an educational psychologist enormously sympathetic to the Chomskian mood of the late 1970s, a time with ideas far removed from those of Leonard Bloomfield. In a widely read article, Olson set his stakes on "consider[ing] what, if anything, is distinctive about written language and to consider the consequences of literacy for the bias it may impart both to our culture and to people's psychological processes" ([1977] 1988, 175). He focused specifically on the written language of schooling, which he described as "essayist prose" or an "autonomous representation of meaning." When children go to school, they find that

> ideally, the printed reader depends on no cues other than linguistic cues; it represents no intentions other than those represented in the text; it is addressed to no one in particular; its author is essentially anonymous; and its meaning is precisely that represented by the sentence meaning. ([1977], 1988, 187)

Both historically and individually, essayist prose, otherwise referred to as "text," evolves from "utterance," the latter term representing oral uses of language. "Text" is strangely disembodied and radically asocial in Olson's universe. No one is involved. Literacy is wholly structures or "linguistic cues."[3]

Olson's cognitive and structuralist biases explain his appeal to ESL theorists, particularly in the late 1970s and early 1980s. Using a combination of Olson and Krashen, Gail Weinstein studied the relationships among schooling, literacy, and second-language acquisition in a group of Hmong. Specifically, she wanted to know why a group of literate, but unschooled, Hmong students acquired English through ESL classes while another nonliterate group of Hmong students did not. Drawing on Krashen's model of second language acquisition, Weinstein contended that the nonliterate Hmong could not comprehend classroom language, and thus acquire English, because of its literate structure. Classroom language, she asserted, both oral and written, is organized much like "essayist-prose." The asocial bias of Olson and Krashen prevented her from asking about the nature of interactions or the purpose of discourses in the classroom. Instead, she focused on linguistic structure.[4]

James Cummins has also relied on Olson (and other theorists with similar arguments) to investigate the role of the first language in the acquisition of English "academic skills" (1979, 3). Cummins divides language use into two categories: communication skills and academic language skills (1979, 4). He also tries "to distinguish those aspects of language proficiency involved in the development of literacy skills" and notes that "these literacy-related aspects are interdependent across languages, i.e., manifestations of a common underlying proficiency" (1979, 3). Cummins prefigures Weinstein as he maintains that "cognitive skills may be more involved in determining the acquisition rate of L2 literacy skills in a classroom context" (1979, 9). Cognitive skills develop along with literacy in the first language.

Cummins relies on an asocial, cognitivist definition of literacy. Cummins begins one piece of research with the claim that he has deliberately tried to "factor out" the "sociocultural determinants" of literacy so that he will be left with what he considers to be the real deal—the "cognitive and linguistic" dimensions of literacy (1979, 34). His sense of literacy is that of David Olson: "A major aim of literacy instruction in schools is to develop students' abilities to manipulate and interpret context-reduced cognitively demanding texts" (1979,15). He also writes that "the dimension of language which is strongly related to literacy skills will be termed 'context-reduced language proficiency' " (1979, 17). He draws from cognitivists Carl Bereiter and Marlene Scardamalia to perceive literacy as "information processing" (1979, 17): "We are proposing instead that the oral language production system cannot be carried over intact into written composition, that it must, in some way, be reconstructed to function autonomously instead of interactively" (1979, 3). What is particularly fascinating about Cummins' work is that it has generated social pedagogies—literacy projects that take into account the students' communities and families—and yet it fosters the wrong explanation as to why these pedagogies work, and why they are important.

Conclusions

In sum, linguistic theory has provided ESL specialists with tacit perspectives on language and its relationship to both second-language acquisition and literacy. These perspectives include claims that: because language is thought, writing is a thinking process; because language acquisition unfolds in the individual, writing is also an individual process; because language is speech, writing is a secondary code, a representation of speech. Generally, when "society" and "social aspects" of language are factored into these frameworks, the equation states that prior to the moment of utterance, society determined language structures, which in turn determined thought. The relationship between language and society is conceived to be unidirectional and static rather than dynamic and dialectical. Because ESL specialists have subscribed to these notions of language, in general, they have precluded the understanding that ESL literacy is a rhetorical act, a social act in which writers and readers interact with other writers and readers, affecting them through language.

Most theorizing about ESL literacy has been carried out by ESL educators for whom the goal of theory is to provide a "scientific" basis for programs through which students can acquire English.

Many ESL specialists equate writing with two distinct activities: practice which promotes language acquisition and composition which occurs only after language structures have been fully acquired. In other words, along with linguistic theory, educational goals have determined ESL specialists' view of literacy as an epiphenomenon of second-language acquisition. Furthermore, because American linguistic theory is fundamentally structuralist, second-language acquisition has often been described, perceived, and in effect defined by the presence or absence of language structures rather than processes. This perspective on second-language acquisition has fostered the idea that literacy is at once a medium, an autonomous skill, and a neutral technology.

The relationship of linguistic theory to concepts of ESL literacy is problematic. ESL specialists have become prisoners of the abstractions of linguistics. Clearly, we can hardly theorize without abstractions, and "terminological screens" (Burke 1962, 471) are necessary for, and in large part the value of, theory. Nonetheless, abstraction becomes destructive when the abstract is reified, when the historical process of abstraction is forgotten, so that abstract descriptions become prescriptions for actual events. This process of reification can be seen in the influence of Bloomfieldian theory on ESL literacy education.

When Bloomfield declared that speech is language and writing is only a representation of speech, he did so to redress a specific historical imbalance in theorizing about language. As stated above, he opposed the elitism he perceived in philological studies based on writing done in European languages. He constructed his theoretical precepts in order to place his project in opposition to that of the philologists and to frame his interest and procedure of describing many American Indian languages that did not have written forms. Bloomfield's abstractions developed dialectically; his interest in analyzing Indian languages required that he develop new descriptive methods and ideological statements, and as he formulated these precepts they influenced his conception of language itself.

When pedagogical grammar writers and language educators of the forties and fifties appropriated Bloomfieldian notions, these principles acquired the status of ontological ideals and lost their sense as historically rooted abstractions and analytical tools. As interest in ESL education and second-language acquisition grew, Bloomfieldian principles became rigid prescriptions for language description and pedagogy. Ironically, while Bloomfield's ideology, understood historically, was originally democratic and egalitarian, it has been used to establish the doctrine that many literacy practices (the study of

English language literature, for example) should be reserved for native speakers while nonnative speakers should focus on the oral uses of language.

In brief, individualist and psychological notions of ESL literacy have been derived from linguistic, and to a lesser degree composition, theory. These conceptions do not adequately represent the whole of ESL literacy practices. In particular, these formulations do not take into account the social processes and organization of literacy practices. They deflect attention from the social constitution of literacy. And, they result in particularly pernicious educational practices.

Notes

1. The word *practice* has three different uses in this book: a) "the practice of education," meaning the actions, skills, and arts of the profession of education, b) "practice" in the ESL class implying that when a student practices English he repeats, he drills, or he does other exercises which will help him to learn the language, c) "literacy practices" meaning the customary, habitual ways in which people read and write in their everyday lives.

2. Exceptions can be found in the work of Thom Heubner and Evelyn Hatch.

3. The literature contains many trenchant critiques of Olson's (Ong, Goody, and others) perspectives on orality and literacy. In particular, I appreciate Deborah Brandt's analysis of the problems with dichotomizing orality and literacy (*Literacy as Involvement: The Acts of Writers, Readers and Texts*, pps. 13–32.)

4. Gail Weinstein-Shr's later work with family literacy projects is discussed in Chapter 5.

Chapter Two

Tacit Theory: Metaphors and Images of ESL Literacy

ESL specialists presume that their ideas about literacy are "scientific" and "objective" because they are drawn from linguistics. They also believe that they express these ideas in transparent and ideologically neutral language. But if we examine the language of ESL theory carefully, we find a surplus of meaning; the metaphors and images of theory harbor their *own* theories and ideologies of literacy. Scrutinizing not only the methodology but also the rhetoric of research is crucial for ESL teachers because metaphors reveal patterns of thought and feelings that not only reflect but also constrain interactions in the ESL literacy classroom. The beliefs that educators and researchers hold about literacy set up and mediate the literacy practices themselves.

Among educators, writers, and researchers there are two primary yet conflicting stories about ESL literacy: some believe that ESL literacy practices enable writers and readers to transcend local and often parochial social interactions; others contend that ESL literacy practices mediate social and political domination. Educators and linguists promote ESL literacy with the former ideology and ESL students and writers, those subjects in neocolonial social positions, often resist ESL literacy by maintaining the latter argument.

These two ideologies need not be mutually exclusive or antinomic; they may be conceived as related dialectically. The educator can envision and teach literacy practices so that ESL students and writers can resist English, or the domination enacted through English, and create their own ESL literacy practices which result in multi-ethnic communication. In Bakhtin's words, "Such a dialogic encounter does not result in mixing and merging" (*Speech Genres* 7). This is not The Three Bears theory of literacy, suggesting that the middle, not too hot and not too cold, is "just right." In this dialectic, both ethnicity and universalism are right, but only when the possibility exists for both.

ESL Literacy and the Myth of Babel

The metaphors which surround ESL literacy are reminiscent of the myth of Babel. This is hardly coincidence. Throughout the twentieth (and soon the twenty-first) century, linguists have posed questions about the causes and consequences of linguistic diversity. In late nineteenth-century American linguistics, D. W. Whitney used the myth of Babel to explore the meaning of multilingualism:

> Out of the congeries of jarring tribes are growing great nations; out of the Babel of discordant dialects are growing languages of wider and constantly extending unity. The two kinds of change go hand in hand, simply because the one of them is dependent on the other. . . . ([1875] 1980, 176)

Whitney believed that as "civilization" grew, fewer languages would be spoken. He clearly disdained the linguistic diversity of the "tribes." He hoped that the "cultivated languages" would eliminate the "patois":

> So, if by external forces, every act and influence of which is clearly definable, the cultivated languages have been and are extending their sway, crowding out of existence the patois which had grown up under the old order of things, gaining such advantage that men are beginning to dream of a time when one language may be spoken all over the earth. And though the dream may be Utopian, there is not an element of the theoretically impossible in it; only a certain condition of external circumstances is needed to render it inevitable. ([1875] 1980, 176)

Yet, he acknowledged that a single "cultivated" language may "extend [its] sway" through "external circumstances," or less euphemistically through "external forces." This force, whatever it may consist of, could be justified because it would bring about a Utopian dream—"a time when one language may be spoken all over the earth" (Whitney [1985] 1980, 176).

Unlike Whitney, contemporary ESL theorists do not refer directly to Babel. Their attitudes toward ESL literacy parallel the myth. In Babel, language and social relations are in a dialectic relationship of mutual influence. In discussions of ESL literacy, remnants of the myth abound because the problem of multi-lingualism underlies all ESL theory.

Using Babel to interpret the metaphors of ESL, we arrive at two tacit theories of ESL literacy.

Theory One: The Universalist Theme of Transcendence

In the Kabbalist interpretation of Babel, the tower was built so that the tribe of Shem could reach the heavens. At this time humanity had but one language. This universal language was derived from the tongue that Adam had used to name the objects of Eden. In this Adamic language, words mapped directly, perfectly onto objects, putting humans in direct contact with reality. Name and essence bore a necessary and internal relation to each other; the name did not merely denote but was the actual essence of its object. Because neither referent nor word could change, there was no linguistic ambiguity, and no diachronic linguistic change. There was no play or poetry with language because a kind of linguistic sublimity had "always already" been achieved.

Also, because Adam's labeling the things of Eden was a speech act analogous to God's speaking the world into being, the Adamic language put men in direct contact with God. The universal language had a third asset: humans could communicate with each other with complete understanding. Language did not mediate; it was "like a flawless glass through which a light of total understanding flowed" (Steiner 1975, 189). In other words, when humans spoke but one language, they were in a threefold state of grace: they knew reality; they knew God; they knew each other.

When the tribe of Shem was castigated for its arrogant attempt to build a tower reaching the heavens, its punishment was henceforth to inhabit linguistically distinct communities. According to the Kabbalists, multiple languages were forced upon the tribe of Shem so that the members of the tribe could not understand each other and finish the tower. After multiplying the tribe's languages, God scattered the people over the globe. Even sociolinguists have been attracted to the explanatory power of this myth. Einar Haugen, for example, reverses the logic of Babel to argue that because the tribe was disseminated, the members began to speak different languages (1973, 47–56).

Many of the metaphors used to describe ESL literacy are reminiscent of this interpretation of Babel. These metaphors express a universalist philosophy: the world's multiplicity of languages is a punishment and a curse. Multilingualism created linguistic misappprehension. With and only with linguistic diversity did language fall from oneness with reality to become a mediator of reality, polysemous at best, cacophonous at worst. From the universalist perspective, English literacy is a kind of universal language that will recreate understanding.

The argument for using English as a "world" or "international" language is full of universalist ideology which, in turn, is used as a rationale and motivation for teaching ESL. To the extent that English does mediate global communication, English becomes an analogue of a lost, original, and universal language. Those who use English internationally move toward recuperating a Utopian language.

The universalist also claims that English can help create national and global communities. Some proponents of ESL contend that English, and English literacy in particular, has the capacity to unite people "against divisive tendencies inherent in the multiplicity of . . . languages within the same geographic state" (Ngũgĩ 1986, 6). Some would argue that English as the language of government, trade, and schooling will save the day for postcolonial nations with little cultural or linguistic coherence. In English these nations hope for a "politically neutral language beyond the reproaches of tribalism or colonialism" (Ngũgĩ 1986, 6). English is assumed to be the "natural language of literary and even political mediation between . . . people in the same nation and between nations . . . and other continents" (Ngũgĩ 1986, 6). Within this scheme, literacy practices themselves are endowed with the capacity to develop community and build nations.

English has additional benefits; it provides a path to transcend the limits of remote locales and little known languages. Along these lines, some educators actually promote ESL as an escape from a "cultural cocoon"; in the words of Kenneth Chastain "stepping outside one's own language is liberating" (1976, 5).

Although universalists suggest that English literacy mediates global unity, their argument develops in strikingly, but not surprisingly, abstract and ahistorical directions. Universalist proponents of ESL write as though English literacy practices were a culturally neutral unifier and universalizer among peoples. ESL literacy practices are disembodied from all social circumstances and English itself is looked upon as if it had become an international language by accident. Some of the most extreme universalists write that English is especially suited for global use because of its "plasticity" (Senghor, quoted in Bailey 1983, 32) or its "intrinsic economy or efficiency" (Bailey 1983, 31).

Universalists represent English literacy as a key to the international world of science and technology. Yet, this world itself is abstract and perhaps even uninhabited. Science has no history, technology no humans. English is a container for "objective" discourse, "methods of inquiry," and "scientific concepts." This perspective on particular language uses is not surprising given the ways in which linguists prize the idea that their discipline is an objective "science" without ideology. English provides access to science and technology, a universe unsullied by history and social interaction.

Within the framework of this ideology, ESL literacy is pictured as functioning mechanistically. Whereas intersubjective metaphors describe reading and writing as a type of social interaction or negotiation between author and reader with the text as mediator, the universalists portray writers and readers much like machines, specifically like computers. ESL readers and writers encode and decode. They extract information from texts.

The universalists discount history. When they do acknowledge that English has become a world language through colonialism, they also maintain that the history of ESL is irrelevant. English, like the tower of Babel, can rise above particular historical exigencies. In this representation, a world language is seen to bring such benefits that amnesia sets in, and the ESL learners forget that English was the language of their colonizers. Even such a wise sociolinguist as Joshua Fishman has fallen into this ideological web. He argues:

> Attitudinal resistance to English can be expected to weaken as younger generations successively shed more and more of the puristic and exclusivistic ideologies that their parents and teachers formulated and espoused during the formative struggles for political and cultural independence. . . . [I]ncreased acquisition and improved attitudes toward English as an additional language are likely, particularly in technological contexts. (1980, 308–9)

Fishman recognizes that European colonizers imposed English in many parts of the world, but he writes as though independence absolved English of any colonial past. In postcolonial times, language becomes an oddly neutral medium, separated from history, politics, and social processes in general. Fishman discusses the process of learning to "like" English "as an additional language" without envisioning or documenting how actual interactions, would result in the "improved attitudes." In Fishman's discussion, learners "shed" their bad attitudes toward English, like a bird molts old feathers. Innocent of politics and economics, English as an international language provides at least a partial antidote to the linguistic fall from grace.

Educators who write about ESL literacy draw not only theoretical biases but also many of their ideological turns from their linguistic training. While promoting interest in the multiplicity of human languages, the work of early American structuralist linguists often revealed a deep underlying repugnance to this diversity. The structuralist enterprise projected an idealized systematicity for language. Structuralist linguists, of both the French and American traditions, avoided the subject of linguistic variation. Since Ferdinand de Saussure, they have programmatically studied not "parole," or actual utterances, but "langue," an idealized construct in which variation and change disappear. While linguists uniformly recognize that languages are diachronically ever-changing and synchronically variant, few, it seems, can bear to witness the change and variation directly. They reify languages. Babel seems to haunt even the "science" of linguistics. Although sociolinguists specifically aim to analyze linguistic variation, they still have a tendency to hypostatize specific languages and language itself (Martinet in Haugen 1972, iv). Linguistics becomes a conceptual opponent to thinking about multilingualism.

Much as in Babel, the varying and variant language of the multilingual threatens the universalist, structuralist picture of a language as a firm and stable system. Even in the heyday of structuralism, when sociolinguist Einar Haugen began to examine the language of bi- and multilinguals, he was forced to question the basic precepts and terms of modern structuralist linguistics:

> Language is probably not a closed system at all, but a complex congerie of interacting systems, open at both ends, namely the past and the future. Its 'synchronic' present may only be a function of what it has been and will be. Perhaps a close analysis of these ragged margins of linguistic behavior will yield significant information concerning the nature of language itself. (1972, 77)

From the bilinguals' "ragged margins of language use" Haugen was able to see that a language is a fiction, a construct even though the structuralist project had removed from sight the loose edges of any given language. It could even be postulated that the structuralist program, in its search for universals, was driven to neutralize the implications of Babel: that human language would permanently be plagued with diversity, and that, as a result, human language would never be transparent. Because they view linguistic unity as Utopian, universalists dread linguistic variation. It is as though they fear that unchecked linguistic diversity will obliterate languages as we know them, resulting in the Babelian tragedy of humans scattered into isolated monads of linguistic solipsism.

Because of their training in structural linguistics, educators promote ESL literacy practices as a kind of universal language which promises, in turn, a proverbial return to Eden. Many ESL writers, however, tell a different story.

Interpretation Two:
The Ethnicist Theme of Transgression

A second interpretation of Babel reveals an opposing view of multilingualism and, by extension, of ESL literacy practices. In this reading of Babel, the tribe of Shem constructed the tower not to reach the heavens but rather to impose its language or "lip" on the world. If they had succeeded, it would have been "by violent hegemony over the rest of the world" (Derrida 1985, 101). They would not have recreated a lost Utopian monolingualism. Instead, there would have been a particular language imposed by force:

> It would not have been a universal language to which everyone would have had access. Rather the master with the most force would have imposed this language on the world and, by virtue of this fact, it would have become the universal tongue. (Derrida 1985, 101)

This reading of Babel challenges the basic tenets of the universalist ideology, stressing that there can be no Utopian universal language. Dreams of a monolingual world rationalize violent transgressions. A single language comes to be used in a wide region of the world only when one group dominates and oppresses another. In this version of Babel, the tribe of Shem is condemned for attempting to force its language on the world.

Many ESL writers corroborate this second interpretation of Babel. They see English as the language of Shem. They maintain what I will call the ethnicist position: ESL literacy practices result from the Other dominating "us"; they constitute capitulation to this Other. All uses of a language other than the mother tongue endanger "us" or "our people"; the mother tongue constitutes the identity of a people—their ethnicity. ESL literacy practices are nefarious, and both the ESL reader/writer and the native English speaking community are treacherous.

The ethnicist position was recognized by Fishman when he wrote about learners' "attitudinal resistance" to English. He also acknowledged that learners' "exclusivistic" feelings about their mother tongues were formed when their countries were fighting for independence from English-speaking colonizers. However, contrary to Fishman's predictions, learners' fondness for English is not growing. In some countries, governments aim to protect the autonomy of local communities by restricting the uses of English. The logic is that if an Other language can be confined, so can the Other, and "we" will thus be protected from potential transgressions. Kenyan writer Ngũgĩ wa Thiong'o resists the Other by denouncing English. In 1986, he began a book of literary criticism with the statement that it is his "farewell to English as a vehicle for any of [his] writings" (2). "I believe that my writing in Gikuyu language, a Kenyan language, an African language is part and parcel of the anti-imperialist struggles of Kenyan and African peoples" (28).

In a poem entitled "Rape Report" Rita Urias Mendoza writes:

> He pushed down and tried to force me to give in. . . . He received praise for what he did to me. He took something that was sacred and beautiful to me and replaced it with four-letter words. I am making this report in English, you see, I've been raped of my native tongue. (1988, 1)

Mendoza is a victim. She suggests that there is no way to win in this arena of violence. Even as she writes a poem (in English) about writing a rape report in English, she is saying that using English is profane if not completely empty. The content of her writing and her stated ideology about her writing are contradictory. But she is not duplicitous; both positions are called for in the very real histories of Hispanic immigrants to the United States. To be heard by the dominant society, they must use English even though they protest against this linguistic domination.

The ethnicist ideology reveals a desire to restore and/or preserve the local community. Chicano critic Tomás Rivera states that this "deep need for community reflects a colonized mind." Writing, he claims, can recuperate the "diffused tribe or nation" (1982, 10). But only in the mother tongue can literacy provide a remedy for diaspora. Substantiating Rivera's claims, Chicano writer Miguel M. Méndez explains why he writes in Spanish rather than English:

> Spiritually I identify totally with the Spanish language. I believe that language is the structure on which all culture rests. If the language disappears, there remain memories that, as they slowly fade away, take the ancestral culture into oblivion. In our case, the Spanish language is the most powerful factor with respect to a means of identity. I believe that Spanish is essential to us; if we leave it behind, we risk developing an unsure character. Spanish is our geneological language, in a manner of speaking; if we forget it we will lose many memories that are proper to our historical nature and then we will be culturally poor without the authenticity that a culture gives through the centuries. (1980, 87–8)

Language and literacy mediate identity, especially ethnic and community identity. A common language allows people to construct a common narrative, a history, that forms the basis of their cultural awareness. Stories make ethnic and community identity concrete. Ngũgĩ believes that English breaks the connections among language, culture, and ethnic identity. English can

> annihilate a people's belief in their names, in their languages, in their environment, in their heritage of struggle, in their unity, in their capacities and ultimately in themselves. It makes them see their past as one wasteland of nonachievement and it makes them want to distance themselves from that wasteland. It makes them want to identify with that which is furthest removed from themselves. (1985, 3)

For Ngũgĩ, English is far from a mediator of Utopia. English "annihilates," like a "bomb."

Ngũgĩ envisions this destruction as far more than figurative. He argues that English has had devastating economic consequences for local communities. When the colonialists imposed English, their real aim was to "control the people's wealth: what they produced, how they produced it, and how it was distributed" (1985, 16). In *Decolonizing the Mind* he powerfully protests that English was the key to the mental domination necessary for the colonizers to exploit the African economy. In Ngũgĩ's words "the domination of a people's language by the languages of the colonizing nations was crucial to the domination of the mental universe of the colonized" (1985, 16).

If the universalists believe that literacy has particular powers to create global community, the ethnicists find in literacy a potent form of oppression. Ngũgĩ argues that literacy practices provide "the most effective area of domination":

> The language of an African child's formal education was foreign. The language of the books he read was foreign. . . . There was often not the slightest relationship between the child's written world, which was also the language of his schooling, and the world of his immediate environment in the the family and the community. For a colonial child, the harmony existing between the three aspects of language as communication was irrevocably broken. (1985, 17)

Colonially "imposed" languages could never completely eliminate the native tongues. But the colonialists could control the institutions of schooling and impose their languages totally in the literacy taught there. The oral native tongue of the home came to be connected to the "harmony" of Utopia. English and literacy became associated with oppression because schools were institutions of the colonizers. The children's social worlds were bifurcated. School and home were different linguistic realms.

Schooling and ESL literacy practices created a cadre of African teachers, students, secretaries, and bureaucrats in neo- or post-colonial governments. This was, in many ways, a new social class—a petite bourgeoisie which lacked its own traditions even though it had "uneasy roots . . . in the culture of the peasantry." ESL literacy became a second order colonization as novelists from this same new social class began to portray the peasantry and working class of Africa as English speaking. While this image of Africans is ersatz, it resulted in illusory social consciousness, a sense of history and social community for the English-speaking petite bourgeoisie. Not surprisingly Ngũgĩ cries out against "clear negation or falsification of the historical process and reality" (1985, 22). Again, the ethnicist argues that English literacy destroys true community offering a sham in its place.

Lies and transgression are associated with nonnative literacy in the novel *Shame* by Salman Rushdie. Through metaphor Rushdie suggests that nonnative writers are criminals in the eyes of their own community, the community of their mother tongue. Accusations are hurled:

> Poacher! Pirate! We reject your authority. We know you, with your
> foreign language wrapped around you like a flag: speaking about us
> in your forked tongue, what can you tell but lies? (1983, 23)

Language is property that can be poached and pirated away. A "foreign" language makes an Other of the writer, a *"you"* speaking about *"us."* The writer is not accepted as an "author." Her or his writing is not only perfidious, it is mendacious. The second-language writer is suspect, without authority.

Ngũgĩ and Rushdie are hardly idiosyncratic in their disavowal of nonnative literacy. Even writers using ESL express the ethnicist sense that the enterprise is damned. Some argue that true creativity is not possible in ESL literacy. Morbidity and antisepsis permeate Nigerian novelist and critic Obi Wali's sense of ESL writing: "Until these writers and their Western midwives accept the fact that any true African literature must be written in African languages, they would be merely pursuing a dead end, which can only lead to sterility, uncreativity and frustration" (1963, 10). English is midwife to mendacity. Only in one's mother tongue is truth or "true literature" expressible. Menghistu Lemma, an Ethiopian dramatist, takes Wali's argument one step further, attributing nearly mystical qualities to the first language. He argues against writing in English, saying that "people dream in their own language, language deeply embedded in the unconscious of a people" (quoted in Gerard 1971, 375).

Many ESL writers describe their discomfort in psychological terms, while others reveal that inhibiting social relationships are the foundations of second language literacy. Chicano authors are described as "newcomers to the culture" by Méndez M., and Africans writing in English are spoken of as "tourists" by Lemma. As a legacy of Babel, ESL writers are seen as neophytes, students and novices. Metaphors reveal the absence of authority and social equality attributed to ESL literacy practices. These writers judge themselves and are judged by others this way because in truth they have acquired English in circumstances in which they were not in power or control. The social conditions of literacy and its acquisition constitute the literacy practices themselves.

The problem with the ethnicist position is that all too often language itself becomes the villain rather than the social interactions in which language and literacy are used and acquired. Ngũgĩ provides use with an example. He was presented with English literacy in school, as are most ESL literates. As English was introduced, Ngũgĩ's mother tongue was suppressed, and the entire process was particularly heinous:

> One of the most humiliating experiences was to be caught speaking Gikuyu in the vicinity of the school. The culprit was given corporal punishment—three to five strokes of the cane on bare buttocks—or was made to carry a metal plate around the neck with inscriptions such as I AM STUPID or I AM A DONKEY.... [C]hildren were turned into witchhunters and in the process were being taught the lucrative value of being a traitor to one's immediate community. (1985, 11)

This "systematic suppression" of Gikuyu was accompanied by "the elevation of English," so that

> [o]rature (oral literature) in Kenyan languages stopped. In primary school I now read simplified Dickens and Stevenson alongside Rider Haggard. Jim Hawkins, Oliver Twist, Tom Brown—not Hare, Leopard and Lion—were now my daily companions in the world of imagination. (1985, 13)

To these interactions, Ngũgĩ attributes the following meaning: "... language and literature were taking us further and further from ourselves to other selves, from our world to other worlds" (1985, 12). With this assertion, Ngũgĩ embarks into the ideology of Babel. He inaugurates the "we"/Other dynamic which is characteristic of ethnicity. But most importantly, he proposes that this relationship is created by English literacy. What Ngũgĩ finally claims is that the use of English, when it is an "alien" language, engenders the oppression and psychological domination of its users. English itself, he claims, colonizes the mind, is a "means of spiritual subjugation," "[holding] the soul prisoner." He also contends that this process of "subjugation" occurs because "the language of conceptualization was foreign [to the African child]. Thought, to him, took the visible form of a foreign language" (1985, 17).

Ngũgĩ proposes that English literacy per se oppresses. Here, his reasoning is similar to theorists like Walter Ong and David Olson who seem to suggest that literacy, in the sense of the printed word, effects cognition. While the educational practices that Ngũgĩ describes are intended to control the Kenyan students, it is not English, the language, that effects oppression, but the interactions through which English literacy is introduced and maintained. Ngũgĩ's analysis assumes that the characteristics of social processes are isomorphic with, and perhaps somehow transferred to, the psychological plane.

Conflicts of Ethnicity and Universalism

The ethnicist and universalist positions are ideological. The ethnicist resists the power of English speakers; the universalist justifies the dominance and control. Yet, these positions are also idealized constructs. In reality, most discussions of ESL literacy incorporate terms and occasionally even conflicting conclusions from both points of view. Universalist and ethnicist sensibilities commingle; neither ideology is found in an unalloyed form. Many writers and educators seem to struggle with antonymous impulses—to promote both linguistic diversity and uniformity, monolingualism and multilingualism, univocality and polyphony. For many this double vision of ethnicity and universalism creates a discourse that appears ridden with contradictory, competing claims.

Richard Rodríguez' essays about learning English are marked by just such an unresolved jangle of ideas and feelings. What makes Rodríguez' ideas so singularly disturbing is that he promotes the universalist ideology along with his own pain in learning English. While universalists usually do not acknowledge that loss may be incurred by taking on a second language, Rodríguez displays his alienation from his mother tongue community as though it were a medal conferred for courage in battle.

He describes his use of English through metaphors found in the ethnicist tale of Babel: tropes of loss, transgression, and thievery. His very title *Hunger of Memory* evokes Méndez M.'s argument that ESL literacy erodes memories which constitute the narratives of mother-tongue culture. Claiming that "I couldn't believe the English language was mine to use," Rodríguez echoes the ethnicist notion that the mother tongue is only and all that is properly "ours" (1982, 30). The Other language is the property of the Other.

Rodríguez did not see himself as a criminal, but he did, as a child, believe that he had committed "a sin of betrayal by learning English" (1982, 30). He agrees with Ngũgĩ that ESL literacy education shatters a child's linguistic Eden, the world conceived in the mother tongue. While Ngũgĩ finds this education oppressive and devastating, personally and culturally, Rodríguez says he finds it liberating. For Ngũgĩ the solution to Babel is in resistance to ESL; for Rodríguez the mother tongue community is not a home but a prison:

> I couldn't believe that Spanish was a public language, like English. Spanish speakers, rather seemed related to me, for I sensed that we shared through our language—the experience of feeling apart from los gringos. It was a ghetto Spanish that I heard and I spoke. Like those whose lives are bound by a barrio, I was reminded by Spanish of my own separateness from los otros, los gringos in power. (1982, 16)

Rodríguez wants to believe that power comes from adopting the language of "los gringos." He reasons that Spanish limited his social relations and thus his access to power. When Rodríguez came to be literate in English, he found "a vast public identity" (1982, 81). His language betrays the universalist's optimism that ESL will mediate his separateness, his life "bound by a barrio," but he also acknowledges that ESL is not a neutral language. It is the language of "los gringos in power."

Rodríguez would agree with the ethnicist charge that taking on a second language will change the relationships in which one is involved:

> The great change in my life was not linguistic but social. If after becoming a successful student, I no longer heard intimate voices as often as I had earlier, it was not because I spoke English rather than Spanish. It was because I used public language for most of the day. I moved easily at last, a citizen in a crowded city of words. (1982, 32)

First a student, then a citizen, Rodríguez characterizes his success in terms of social roles. More precisely, he appears to argue that the social relationships themselves, as mediated by English, are what changed his life. Rodríguez appeals to a huge audience. It is hard to completely discount the tale he spins. He acknowledges the pain of learning a second language. He speaks of the hungers that his loss of memory has brought. He even grants that English speakers are the ones with power. Yet, he does not advocate the ethnicist resistance to ESL literacy. Instead, he composes his own version of the Horatio

Alger story. Rodríguez concludes that all the pain and loss are "worth it"; unlike Méndez M. and Lemma, he is neither a tourist nor a newcomer in the world of ESL literacy. He writes of the beauty of his well earned citizenry, but if we throw his tale in an acid bath, in its bony remains, we will find that what Rodríguez the universalist has really earned is financial success in his newfound world. One wonders what he would argue if he had not sold so many books.

Obviously ESL literacy practices call forth both ethnicist and universalist predicates. The conclusions which particular writers, educators, researchers, and so forth arrive at are not random or accidental, however. Their arguments justify their economic positions, their positions and relations to power. Those without power resist and those with power welcome the uses of English literacy.

ESL Literacy Education

ESL literacy pedagogy is also fraught with contradictory positions. While ESL educators have justified their programs as "scientifically based" on the principles of structural linguistics (see Chapter 1), their stances are, in fact, highly ideological, highly political.

As ESL educators began to formalize writing pedagogy, it became almost universally accepted that the ESL writer had to be "controlled." The program of controlled composition that was instituted in ESL classes sought to prohibit "free expression" until the writer could use English in a native-like or nearly "error-free" fashion. As William Slager noted in 1966, "The assumption, by now basic to the profession, is that composing—writing beyond the sentence level— must be guided or preferably controlled" (232). Because a stage of error-free writing never arrived for many students, control was often extended throughout their ESL education.

Control and freedom metaphors run throughout ESL educators' ideas about literacy pedagogy. These metaphors support the ethnicist sense that ESL literacy amounts to one group, the one "owning" the language being imposed, possessing power and using it to control the Other, the second-language users. As in the events of Babel, the group with force has imposed its language on the weaker Other.

In his early work, Robert Kaplan argued for a more subtle form of control, a negation of the ESL writers' authority. He maintained that "it is necessary for the nonnative speaker learning English to *master* the rhetoric of the English paragraph" but "creativity and imagination" were not to be the concern of the ESL literacy class. "The English class must not aim too high"; "imitation . . . is the sought aim" ([1966], 1972, 261, emphasis added).

In his efforts to rationalize restricted uses of English literacy for nonnative speakers, Kaplan quotes from Edward Sapir, the linguist most famous for theorizing about connections between the form of a language and the culture of a people. Ironically, although Kaplan undoubtedly believes in the value of ESL literacy, this quotation is in the nomenclature of Ngũgĩ and other ethnicists' arguments damning the entire enterprise of ESL literacy:

> An oft-noted peculiarity of the development of culture is the fact that it reaches its greatest heights in comparatively small, autonomous groups. In fact, it is doubtful if a genuine culture ever properly belongs to more that (sic) a restricted group, a group between the members of which there can be said to be something like direct intensive spiritual contact. . . . A narrowly localized culture may, and often does, spread its influence far beyond its properly restricted sphere. Sometimes it sets the pace for a whole nationality, for a far flung empire. It can do so, however, only at the expense of diluting the spirit as it moves away from its home, of degenerating into an imitative attitudinizing. (Sapir, quoted in Kaplan [1966], 1972, 261)

Kaplan uses Sapir to make points with which the ethnicists would agree; although Sapir is speaking of the limits of culture, language is conflated with culture. Accordingly, Kaplan can use Sapir to talk about the limits of a language. He seems to say that some uses of a language should be left to native speakers. He, like Méndez M., believes in a spiritual connection between creativity, the mother tongue, and its community. This rhetoric is used as a rationale for limiting if not controlling what the student is allowed to write, however. If the uses of a language are limited, then it is the native speakers who can decide who can use it and how it should be used. The student will be a "master" of the English paragraph by fiat of the teacher. It is not up to the student, the learner, the nonnative speaker to decide how, when, and where to use English literacy; the linguist and educator know best. And they dictate the English which the student must "control"; finally, they, not the student, remain master. (Some ESL literacy educators have, of course, become aware of this and revised their practices. See examples in Chapter 5.)

After Babel, English education has functioned in two complementary ways: first, to standardize English, to unify it; second, to protect and ensure this unity and to spread English as the language of a people of power and force. Notions of standards and protection for English have informed many readings of ESL writing.

Teachers apparently feel charged with mitigating the ESL writers' potential for linguistic destruction. Critic A. Afolayan believes that education must protect English from fragmentation into dialects:

> There has been considerable interaction among the various peoples
> of Nigeria . . . [who] have tended to acquire a common model
> of intelligible English. This tendency has been helped by the influ-
> ence of national educational agencies . . . [which] have helped to
> build up a tradition of correctness in English usage throughout the
> country. (1971, 56)

Euphemistically, Afolayan talks about educational agencies and
their influence "to build up a tradition of correctness." With these
abstractions, he avoids talk of teachers' control over students or student writing. He dodges the issues of politics and ideology implicit
in the social relations between ESL teachers and students. Clearly, he
wants to uphold a standard of "correctness" for Nigerian English,
and he writes as though his support for English correctness were
perfectly scrupulous.

Generally readers assume that ESL writers have meant for
their language to match, as nearly as possible, some native speaker
variety, generally an English from Britain or the United States. ESL
educators almost always read student writers with these assumptions. Even teachers with training in linguistics may find ESL students culpable of "destroying" the language. They are particularly
suspect as writers; their "spoilage" moored on paper appears in-
effaceable. (See Chapter 6 for more discussion of reading ESL writing.) Moreover, second language writers may force a reader, a
linguist, a literary critic, or a teacher to confront a lack of "presence,"
to appropriate Derrida's terms, in language. ESL speakers are one
step removed from logos and presence; second-language writers are
behind two veils, creating a kind of "trace" to the second power. Not
only student writing but also published authors are interpreted this
way as well.

A. Afolayan reads Nigerian novelist Amos Tutuola as though he
were a student. He describes the language of Tutuola's early novel
The Palm-Wine Drinkard as that of a pupil of "post-primary education at approximately the level of present-day Secondary Class Two."
In Tutuola's last novel, his language has apparently "improved"
because it is characterized as the language of "a user with the Secondary Class Four education" (1971, 54). According to Afolayan,
Tutuola's style results from an *"inadequate teaching program"* (1971,
54, emphasis added); in Tutuola's work, Afolayan finds "elementary
grammar mistakes . . . which a sounder education in English would
have removed" (1971, 55). This way of reading deprives the writer of
authority. He is no longer an adult; he is a childlike pupil who waits
for his teacher's corrections. Imbued with power, the reader rather
than the writer has become the true author of the text. While writing
the ESL text, this reader recreates his place in the lineage of Shem.

Many readers focus only on the acceptability or correctness of the language of the ESL writer. Often judgments of a writer's language are based on what readers know about a writer's educational background. Much like Afolayan, John Povey asserts that the prose of Amos Tutuola "can be called inaccurate and at worst simply illiterate." Tutuola, Povey points out, "had only minimal schooling and his English is faulty in the extreme" (1969, 85). While he acknowledges that Tutuola's "neologisms and variants seem to add meaning and emphasis to the writer's words," Povey remains disturbed because "Tutuola's prose seems to *defy* any normal structural analysis based upon standard English" (1969, 85). The language of this criticism is transparently ideological—the native speaking reader is upset when the ESL writer defies.

In contrast to the unschooled writer, Povey portrays the writing of "well-educated men" as

> not the simple aping of a foreign style, with accidental errors, but the molding of the language to recognizable individual styles and idioms. (1969, 84)

The unschooled writer apes and has accidents, not very attractive images, while those who have been educated can shape or "mold" their language to an individual style.

Style in ESL literacy is a particularly slippery issue The writers unschooled in the canon of British and American literature are seldom and begrudgingly credited with style. More often than not, readers comment on errors and mistakes, stealing again the writers' potential for intention and authority. Critic John Povey is confused and vexed about the issue of standards and style as he writes about the language of the pamphlets literature and popular novels of the Nigerian town of Onitsha. He sees evidence in these works of "linguistic degeneration" (1969, 87). Yet, he sums up their value with this contradictory epithet—they "display an inferior but individualistic and effective English" (1969, 86).

Tutuola's writing, it must be remembered, was described as defying structural analysis. Gabriel Okara, however, is a writer who "belongs to the group holding advanced degrees in English literature," so critic Povey decides that Okara is "aware that he is *heir* to a wide tradition of English literature" (1969, 83–4, emphasis added). In Okara's writing Povey finds "a highly mannered style charged with an intensity which sets it far from anticipated modern diction with its aim at low-keyed direct and natural language for its effects" (1969, 92).

Okara, however, claims no such style for himself. He characterizes his work as "virtually a direct translation from [the] mother tongue Ijaw" (1973, 138). In addition, while novelist Cyprian Ekwensi has a degree in Pharmacy, he has limited formal study of English literature. Ekwensi's work is read as an example of "the dangers inherent in the second hand borrowing from dubious sources" (Povey 1969, 88). Apparently, without formal education, the writer cannot learn to distinguish the appropriate models after which to fashion his prose. This same reader compares Ekwensi to Chinua Achebe who has "formal literary training." Achebe, the critic believes, "enriches the formal English which he has borrowed" (Povey 1969, 94).

Educators, literary critics, and researchers read the writing of nonnative speakers with a protective eye and ear. When an individual heir to the canonical literary tradition writes in ESL, they gaze and listen in admiration. When the unschooled individual publishes in ESL, they may tolerate the "neologisms," while hoping that the writer's language will improve. When a group creates its own English and its own literacy practices, its pamphlet literature in a regional dialect, readers harshly dismiss the "linguistic degeneration" that has occurred. For Povey, educated writers' styles are most palatable, at least in part, because they are "individual," not in "demand as a local model of English" (1969, 82); the assumption is that education will have tempered these writers' abilities to create a new and variegated English. They have in Povey's view accepted their positions as "borrowers" of English because they have been steeped in its tradition.

Readers best tolerate, it seems, the ESL writer who least threatens the tower of unified English. Our ways of reading the writing of ESL students ward off our fears of Babel—that with freedom for ESL writers, communication will falter, solipsism will ensue, and, most cynically that we as readers will have no jobs to do if there is no English to protect.

Ironically, of course, most educators and literary critics are not cynical about ESL literacy. They speak in universalist nomenclature about the promises of ESL literacy:

> From India and Jamaica, from the Philippines and from Pakistan, from Barbados and Korea we find people taking the universality that the English language can give them, and using it to speak to the world through this universal medium. But such is their skill—and perhaps credit must also be given to the supreme flexibility of the English tongue—they are not constricted and inhibited by the forms of the borrowed tongue of a society so far removed from their own . . . [t]hrough it [they can] speak of the universal humanism of people. (Povey 1969, 96)

Typically, ESL educators believe that ESL writers can use a universal medium to write for a universal audience about a universal human condition. They may even be seduced by the extreme universalist notion that the plasticity of English itself is an asset to the ESL writer who is "skilled." Skill is seen as the result of an author's awareness that he is "borrowing" a language, a perception that may, in turn, be a consequence of the author's formal education in the canon of English literature.

The Dialectics of Ethnicity and Universalism

ESL writers have a desire to preserve and create a local community and language and to protect against diaspora and the hegemony of the Other. They also have a drive to restore and create a global community and language and to redress human misunderstandings brought about by language diversity. Rather than recognizing these antonymous pulls and pushes, however, many educators have arrived at a theory of ESL literacy that is replete with contradictions and dichotomies, a discourse which is internally inconsistent. Within the muddled frameworks of these analyses, for instance, a writer "borrows" a "universal language." Obviously, if a language is truly conceived of as "universal," it belongs to all and can be borrowed by none.

A more consistent and powerful theory of ESL literacy would view ethnicity and universalism as related dialectically rather than dichotomously and inimically. It is just such a theory that this book will begin to articulate. Tacit evidence for this theory comes in the work of some researchers, literary critics, ESL writers and educators. While they do not use the word dialectic, their work shows that both the ethnic and the universal culture, language and community can be mediated by ESL literacy. ESL literacy can actually resolve the antinomies between the ethnic and the universal impulses; the universal pushes on the ethnic and the ethnic acts back on the universal. Both pressures are present in their examples of language and literacy practices, producing a synthesis that Chinua Achebe calls a "new voice" (1976, 82), "a world view being defined by writers and artists" according to José Montoya (quoted in Novoa 1980, 131).

Those writers working dialectically abjure the idea that language is the property of a particular group. The ethnicists resisted English because they saw it as belonging to the Other; they also believed that adopting the Other language meant accepting domination by the Other. The dialectical theorists reject the equation of language and property, of language (per se) and domination. "English is not the sole domain of theirs," announced Chicano poet Abelardo Delgado (quoted in Novoa 1980, 104). While Delgado recognizes that "they" exist, apart from "us," language is not the property of its native speakers. There is no tribe of Shem.

The dialectical theorists grant authority to ESL literacy practices. These writers articulate and advocate their own standards and their own styles. Chinua Achebe argues that it is neither "necessary nor desirable" for the second language writer to try to use English "like a native-speaker" (1976, 82). And, further that

> Most African writers write out of an African experience and of commitment to an African destiny. For them that destiny does not include a future European identity for which the present is but an apprenticeship. And let no one be fooled by the fact that we may write in English, for we intend to do unheard of things with it. Already people are worried. (1976, 9)

Moreover, as Achebe indicates above, ESL literacy does not constitute a denial of the mother tongue or the ethnic community. In fact, throughout the essays of *Morning Yet on Creation Day*, Achebe emphasizes that through literacy practices, the African can define his identity and rediscover his history. The stories told through, or mediated by, literacy actually constitute identity and history, as Méndez M. so astutely remarked.

While the ethnicists see language as property, the universalists use organic metaphors to describe the idea of a language. For universalists, English has unity and in this unity resides a life force which has to be protected. ESL literacy is capable of destroying this life unity; multilinguals are described as "the carriers of inter-lingual contagion" for even as innovative a scholar as Einar Haugen (1972, 59). In dialectical theory, however, ESL literacy does not desecrate the language. Writer Gabriel Okara argues:

> Living languages grow like living things, and English is far from a dead language. There are American, West Indian, Australian, Canadian and New Zealand versions of English. All of them add life and vigor to the language while reflecting their own respective cultures. (1973,139)

Even as Okara confirms the universalists' vitalist perspective on language, he does so only to stand up for the ethnicist cause. He concludes that life force enables English to nourish not a universal world order but local, ethnic communities. In Okara both universalist and ethnicist speak.

A dialectic theory argues that the relationship between the writer and English is dynamic; the writer has not only the ability but the right to "do unheard of things with [English]" (Achebe 1976, 9). The relationship among the writer, the mother-tongue, the English-language communities, and English itself is dynamic. Literacy is a human practice through which self, nation, community, and language are defined simultaneously, in a mutually dependent manner. The tower of Babel has not toppled but is forgotten, no longer controlling our imaginations about what ESL literacy can be.

The dialectical theorists differ from the universalists and the ethnicists in the ways that they read ESL writers. This is predictable, of course, because the theories that we harbor about language constrain our readings of texts. Three divergent readings of Gabriel Okara's novel *The Voice* illustrate the idea that reading is not primarily a skill, a neutral, value-free act. Ideology structures meaning. The universalist critic describes Okara as a skilled writer, one able to take a plastic medium, a world language, and express the "human condition" (Povey 1969, 91–2). The ethnicist roundly rebukes Okara for "literary gymnastics" in which he "preys" on his native language, Ijaw, to arrive at a text in English (Ngũgĩ 1985, 8). Okara capitulates, the ethnicist argues, to the oppressor by embracing "a fatalistic logic" that English has "an unassailable position in African literature" (1973, 7). The dialectical reading argues that Okara "uses the white man's language to show his rejection of the white man. The experiment with Ijaw syntax, idioms, and modes of thinking through the medium of English is a realistic assertion of the writer's cultural independence" (Ngara, 56). In this formulation of the dialectic, the two languages, English and Ijaw, are both present, in tension, in Okara's writing, which in turn becomes emblematic of a new social stance and a new culture.

Linguistics has little vocabulary for the sense that both English and the mother tongue are present in ESL literacy. Generally educators read ESL texts as though they were to match a native-speaker's English, usually the very voice, the exact English of the reader. When the text does not fit the voice of the reader, the reader thinks that the writer, consciously or not, has made a mistake—an error. This error is often attributed to the "interference" of the mother tongue. Readers do not interpret this commingling of language and language varieties as positive or as deliberate. Even if educators and critics were to escape the constraints of their training, which has taught them to read for error, for what is not, rather than for what is, they would find no vocabulary with which to talk about the pleasures of such a text.

Some literary critics have given us the sociolinguistic construct of "code-switching" to describe the uses of two languages in a single text. These critics take care to distinguish the switching as a deliberate act, not a mistake; it is in fact rule-governed. The term itself is dichotomous, idealizing the separateness of languages from each other, the unity of individual languages; the terminology itself leads theorists to formulate ethnicist conclusions about ESL literacy practices. One critic states that the switches into English signify "that the alien language of the alien world is being imposed" (Valdés Fallis 1976, 881).

Some literary critics, many of whom are ESL writers themselves, find most interesting the moment of difference in the dialectic. These critics emphasize the process through which the writer or reader realizes the difference between English and the mother tongue and reacts to this difference by pushing against standard English, its uses and its form. These writers may even acknowledge that they aim to subvert the Other and the established order which the standard language mediates. Tino Villanueva asserts that because of the practice of using two languages in the same poem, the aesthetics of Chicano literature are "revolutionary"; through its language, Chicano literature "reevaluates, attacks, and subverts" (Novoa 1980, 261). Francisco Lomelí argues that the Chicano novel "serves a subversive role in its posing of new social orders or undermining established ones" (1982, 38). T. Sifuentes claims that the essay "presents an area of dialogue where the struggle between cultures is the dominant tenor" (1982, 59). And, Ramon Saldívar presents the poststructural articulation of this moment of difference:

> The subversive edge of each of the novels we have examined effects destruction. But this destruction always implies the reconstruction of what has been undone at the site of its former presence. . . . Opting for conflict rather than resolution, for difference over similarity, the Chicano novel is thus not so much the expression of this ideology of difference as it is a production of that ideology. (1979, 88)

The dialectical perspective differs enormously from that of the ethnicists, who resist English to argue for a return to the cradle of the Utopian mother tongue. The ethnicists feel victimized by violence perpetrated against them by English speakers, sometimes in the names of standard English and English literacy. The dialectical thinkers believe that they can use English for their own purposes. This is their ideology.

These critics are aware though that the dialectical moment of antithesis is not static; it is a development in a movement, in a process in time. Other critics are drawn to describe the moment of synthesis in the dialectics of ESL literacy. Juan Bruce Novoa asserts that the two codes are fused, rather than switched. The bilingual writer, he argues, should be thought of as writing "interlingually" (1980, 29). And, unlike Einar Haugen, for Novoa this is a positive ascription, unconnected to "contagion." C. Cárdenas de Dwyer describes the language of the ESL writer as "blended"; it is language, she claims, "which reflects not only the true nature of the Chicano experience, but the linguistic duality which has grown from this emotional, cultural, and philosophical union" (1982, 23). What Novoa and Dwyer are forging is a lexicon that represents ESL style as both a part and a result of a dialectical process.

From poststructuralist anthropologist John Clifford we gather inspiration for a poetics of cultural intervention (1988, 181). He writes of the ways in which the nonnative writer forces readers to confront the limits of their language, or of any single language because nonnative writing eludes an idealized synchronic and stable present. With nonnative writing, the reader must construct readings from "historical and future possibilities." Readers finds themselves in a "hybrid and heteroglot world." Clifford describes this style as one of "neologism" which he claims is radically "indeterminate" (1988, 177). With this writing readers never experience direct linguistic authenticity; the language is transmuted. This is a language of rebellion, a language which can remake a culture.

Chinua Achebe envisions a dialectical synthesis of desires—the fulfillment of both the universal and the ethnic uses of language. He advises that the ESL writer "should aim at fashioning out an English which is at once universal and able to carry his peculiar experience" (1976, 82). Achebe points to a moment in the dialectical process in which the ethnic and the universal are no longer distinguishable, each has turned into the other. English is not theirs, not the ethnic property of a local and powerful community. Rather, English has turned to reveal its universality, it has become a "worldwide language" because it has been pushed "to speak of African experience." This moment is marked by the creation of a "new voice . . . , speaking of African experience in a world wide language" (Achebe 1976, 82). Emmanuel Ngara explicates the dialectical process in terms that complement those of Achebe:

> The success of the African writer will depend on . . . his ability to mould the foreign language into a fit medium for the expression of national culture, national aspirations, the African temperament and the expression of the human predicament as seen through African eyes. (1982, 25)

In spite of their emphasis on synthesis, these writers do not ignore the negative moment of the dialectic, the moment of difference and resistance. Achebe contends that English "submits" to the ESL writers' needs, to the demands for ethnicity. Ngara stresses that the writer must "mould" the language so that it reflects the African as universal and the universal as African (1976, 25).

Dialectics of ESL Literacy Education

Rather than ignoring or suppressing this dialectic of identity and difference, ESL literacy educators could promote it. Ironically it is John Povey who describes how this could be accomplished. The ESL writer is "first encouraged to exploit [English] for his own non-Anglo purposes" (1967, 307). The student "uses his second language by setting it up not as a target which merely allows entry into a foreign culture . . . but as a vehicle of his own [culture]" (1967, 307). The teacher, in other words, deliberately pushes the nonnative student to write differently from native speakers. Povey argues that "The appropriate impulse . . . should not be to join the literary styles which have been established by the American but to express his sense of differentiation and alienation from it" (1967, 307). Students can write bilingual texts and can experiment with code-switching. They can develop a vocabulary for talking about their writing which does not center around the word error, but instead concentrates on the issue of nonnative style. They could splice texts in English with texts from their mother tongues. In Povey's writing program the student is

> encouraged to exploit this language for his own non-Anglo purposes; employing English merely because, if he is to articulate his necessary . . . commitment to the outside world . . . , this is the means he must employ.

Here Povey reaffirms what Ngũgĩ has called a fatalistic (and universalist) logic that English is necessary to get beyond a kind of linguistic prison of the mother tongue. Povey is, on one hand, squarely universalist:

> English does not restrict, it opens up new realms to the writer born into relatively limited linguistic groups. . . . It does not impose a culture but allows the articulation of wide feeling. (1967, 307)

Yet on the other hand, he claims that the ethnicist is "legitimately highly suspicious" of English literacy. He recognizes that nonnative speakers have "non-Anglo purposes" for literacy and nonnative forms of the language as well. The contradictions among goals are resolved by encouraging the writer to use English and resist English simultaneously: the ESL writer is "encouraged to exploit" the language (1967, 307).

Interestingly, the ESL writer's developmental goal is not to compose in a "world language" for a world audience. Rather, in the end, Povey sees this student's language becoming "increasingly sophisticated" and this language use "subsequently allow[ing] him to join the Anglo culture on his own literate and literary terms" (1967, 307).

Finally, English is not a world, a universal language. It is an ethnic language, the tongue of a particular group—the Anglos, a community that the ESL writer will be able to join through his language and literacy practices. In contrast to Povey's ending, a dialectical conclusion to this pedagogy would have the ESL writer changing the communities as he interacts with them through literacy practices.

The myth of Babel has stubbornly haunted our thinking about multilingualism and language diversity. It resonates in our imaginations because it captures some essence of our linguistic desires; it is undoubtedly true that humans do long for a universal transparent language and equally true that human efforts to produce this language mediate struggles for power and economic resources. Simultaneously, people create and maintain community through particular local language and literacy. Educators and critics who ignore either the universalist or the ethnicist motives oversimplify the human linguistic condition. The dialectical theorists discussed above avoid both the feigned innocence of the universalist arguments and the fatalism of the ethnicist contentions. This dialectic provides the basis for a theory of ESL literacy beyond the tales of Shem.

Chapter Three

The Dialectics of ESL Literacy Practices

ESL literacy is best understood as an act which connects readers and writers to others. This contention is probably an obvious one since only wizardlike characters in a world invented by Jorge Luis Borges would choose to write in a second language for themselves alone. Obvious or not, however, this social aspect of ESL literacy is perhaps the least discussed in the field.

In this chapter I will outline a dialectical theory of ESL literacy as a social act. For reasons outlined in previous chapters, my approach differs from the traditional approaches to reading and writing taken in ESL.

Traditional ESL Reading and Writing

From linguistics, ESL specialists have inherited a positivist outlook that has determined methods of research and what counts as legitimate research. This positivist/empiricist perspective suggests that when we investigate a human phenomenon such as language, we will discover—and it is properly our task to discover—its natural and discrete parts. We will also find and describe the already-there-before-our-research essences of the phenomenon and the ways that the object of our analysis works. After we have discovered what is there naturally, we will describe these "findings" in neutral language. This empiricist bias has influenced, in turn, the ways in which ESL literacy practices are taught. There are classes in reading, for example, in which ESL educators teach "comprehension skills," and it is assumed that what it means to comprehend a text is a fairly straightforward matter. In this view, a determinate or predetermined meaning is located in the words and sentences of the text, and teachers can instruct students on methods of finding that meaning. This view of meaning and comprehension is commensurate with a positivist/empiricist perspective on language and language research.

ESL specialists usually divide writing and reading from each other; generally, these activities are studied and taught separately. A course may include writing to practice or test reading comprehension, or a teacher may assign reading as content for writing compositions, but the two remain discrete activities. The boundaries between them are thought to be real. Both break down into skills which may be related but are fundamentally more different than similar.

Skills constitute the whole of these activities—of reading and writing. To understand what writing (or reading) is, you have to know about the skills that comprise it. Development is quantitative and incremental; as a learner gets better at reading and at writing, he has more and more skills.

The field of ESL further divides up instruction and research by taxonomizing texts on the basis of the language or skills presumed to be involved in constructing them. *A Handbook of ESL Literacy,* for example, explains that writing is one of two activities: "the ability to encode speech" and "cognitive writing," or "the ability to express ideas coherently in print, to arrange thoughts logically, and to produce a coherent argument" (1984, 15). In higher education, some researchers have been trying to identify and teach English for Academic Purposes (EAP), which is not really a linguistic code. Rather, the term signifies literacy practices such as summary writing and notetaking. These researchers acknowledge that there may be " 'general reading skills' (such as comprehension)" (Johns 1981, 55), but they question whether and which skills transfer across contexts.

ESL specialists view reading and writing as though they occur *in* a context, as though some essence of reading (or writing) could be extracted out of the context, and this essence of reading would remain intact and would be recognizable as the activity of reading. Readers are more or less able to understand a piece based on contextual factors such as the reader's background knowledge, the social setting in which the piece is read (because this "setting" will influence "affective factors"—motivation, anxiety and so forth). But, neither reading nor writing interact reciprocally with social context. And, of course, reading and writing are primarily mental, psychological, and individual activities. As seen above, even when social factors are taken into account, social behavior is transformed into mental, affective, individual behavior.

Because ESL specialists are concerned with education, they privilege school reading and writing, exercises, compositions, textbooks. Stories, novels, plays, and poems are shunted off as "creative writing," an activity completely distinct from the ESL student writing. This creates a perspective from which ESL teachers might wonder how a description of style in Gabriel Okara's or Amos Tutuola's novels pertains to the writing and instruction of ESL students.

Ironically, in spite of their emphasis on these differences in literacies, ESL specialists seek to isolate some essence, some changeless element beneath the multiplicity of appearance in each of the types of writing and reading that nonnative speakers do. Again, they believe that there is some essence of reading and writing that students use in a context.

Dialectics of ESL Reading and Writing

A dialectical perspective on ESL literacy turns these priorities nearly inside out. First, the term "literacy practices" is substituted for and meant to include both reading and writing. This nomenclature assumes that reading and writing are mutually supporting activities for they involve students in "learning how to mean," using print to explore, expand, and control their worlds (Halliday 1975). Both reading and writing involve composing through language; their microprocesses are similar.

Reading and writing are constituted of social relationships; their macro-processes are also similar. This does not deny a psychological and solitary dimension to ESL literacy practices. Instead the argument is that psychological biases have, by and large, led theorists to ignore the concrete interactions that constitute literacy practices, the activities of groups and pairs, acts which are influenced and controlled by social institutions, such as governments and schools. Literacy practices involve a dialectical merging of individual and social aspects of language: one part cannot exist without another; each part acquires its properties from its relation to the other parts; properties of each evolve as a result of their interpenetration (Levins and Lewontin 1985, 3). This perspective does not ignore micro-processes (such as revision strategies or prediction skills) but instead tries to describe them only in relation to the whole.

Literacy study looks at uses of writing and reading in everyday life. Whereas composing process research envisions a writer alone with his mind and his writing implements, the researcher of literacy practices looks at a whole life and tries to understand the social conditions of the production and uses of texts, their histories. The term literacy stresses the commonalities of many practices of writing and reading: authors and poems, students and compositions, families and notes, governments and tax forms or drivers' licenses. Literacy can and does include writing and reading of technical reports, poems, and grocery lists. From this perspective, when we analyze student literacy and student-literacy instruction, we need to look at all of the social relationships implicated and involved in the writing and reading they do, both in school and out.

The term literacy practices is taken to imply not only a whole, but a dialectical whole, constantly changing, causes becoming effects and effects becoming causes. This approach is highly contextual without separating out context. This distinction may be clarified by looking at the ways in which Shirley Brice Heath talks about literacy and context:

> Literacy events must ... be interpreted in relation to the larger sociocultural patterns which they may exemplify or reflect. For example, ethnography must describe literacy events *in their sociocultural contexts,* so we may come to understand how such patterns as time and space usage, caregiving roles, and age and sex segregation are interdependent with the types and features of literacy events a community develops. (1983, 74, emphasis added)

Here reading and writing are embedded in the workings of everyday life. Yet the relation of context to literacy is unidirectional. Literacy events are situated "in sociocultural contexts" almost as though there would be some way of removing literacy from its contexts as though pen, text, and paper would then constitute literacy. As Elspeth Stuckey argues, it is almost as though literacy were something that could be moved about "transported from scene to scene" like a suitcase (1991, 46). Although Shirley Brice Heath recognizes that "sociocultural patterns" are "interdependent" with literacy, it is not this analysis that she focuses on. She concentrates instead on demarcated entities, or "literacy events" that reflect sociocultural patterns. Interestingly, while Heath does analyze specific instances of interdependence, the terminology of her analysis finally repudiates this interdependence or dialectic.

A dialectical analysis emphasizes that literacy practices are constructed of context. There is no boundary between literacy and context, in other words. The dialectical perspective resists the positivist tendency to hypostatize the object of its analysis. Literacy is a contingent structure in reciprocal relations with its parts. This term describes dynamics rather than things or substances. Accordingly the terms of a dialectical interpretation are relative, signifying relationships rather than entities; a dialectical interpretation avoids reification.

The Dialectics of Ethnicity and Universality

Ethnicity and universality are interpretations that readers and writers form of the relationships between themselves and others— interpretations that are based on discourse (here, of course, we are interested primarily in texts and the discourse that surrounds them) and the social interactions that mediate discourse. Ethnicity and universality are dialectically related. They are relative terms that describe the dynamics of identity and difference that underlie the actions, motives, and social formations constituted by and constitutive of ESL literacy practices. Ethnicity and universalism, therefore, do not signify things or uniform processes but rather they describe changing relationships between writers and readers and texts, cultures, and communities. The concepts of ethnicity and universality cannot be isolated from each other and substantialized, instead they undergo a ceaseless metamorphosis from one to another. It can be said, however, that ethnicity asserts a "we"/Other dynamic and that universality negates or dissolves this assertion.

Through ESL literacy practices, readers and writers develop highly mutable social relationships and interpretations of relationships. If by reading/writing and participating in the social relations that accompany reading and writing, a writer/reader constructs a "we" of ethnicity, she is also imagining an Other. This is not to say that the social relations themselves are imaginary. They are not. But the recognition that I am part of a group, a "we" which necessarily creates an Other, is a mental act. This "we" interpretation of ethnicity is dialectical, a kaleidoscope of changing social relations. Through literacy, the writer/reader may come to believe that more and more people are part of the "we." This writer/reader will be constantly reinvisioning a "we" community. These readers and writers may come to believe that all readers and writers share their interests, that they all belong to the same community. In this case, the dynamic between readers and writers and their texts and communities will have changed so significantly that it is no longer one of ethnicity at all but one of universality. Its referent is constantly transmuting. As the group is being recreated, the "we" can, and in fact frequently does, embrace and subsume fragments of the Other until there may be no Other; there is only a "we," a universal community.

The ethnicists' position that was outlined in Chapter 2 is not dialectical. The purist ethnicists generally assume that the essence of ESL literacy practices is a static "we"/Other dichotomy. The "we" is a stable, salubrious entity, reflecting a primordial unity, a natural "harmony" among self, culture, community, and the mother tongue. They also believe that the "we" is threatened by literacy practices in a second language. Ngũgĩ, for example, envisions the relationship between language and identity to be stable rather than dialectical and dynamic. He argues that "the choice of language and the use to which language is put is central to a people's definition of themselves in relation to their natural and social environment, indeed in relation to the entire universe" (1985, 4). Few would disagree completely that language use is connected to identity. But Ngũgĩ argues for an essential union of self, nation, and mother tongue.

Linguists Ron and Suzanne Scollon have examined how relations of ethnicity mediate ESL literacy. They share with Ngũgĩ a sense that "ethnicity" is a stable entity which depends on language for its preservation. They claim that Athabaskans and native English speakers each employ a "discourse system" that reflects their basic cultural values. In particular, the discourse system reflects and structures interpersonal relations. They contend that if one changes discourse systems, one also changes personality and culture.

The Scollons equate ESL literacy practices with a discourse system that reflects "modern consciousness." Drawing on the ideas of Foucault, and literacy theorists David Olson, Walter Ong, and Jack Goody, the Scollons characterize "modern consciousness" as "a cognitive orientation toward the everyday world including the learning of the world" (1981, 42). In this way of thinking, "this cognitive orientation," texts are "decontextualized in relation to situations" (1981, 49). They argue that

> the ideal [essayist] text is closed to alternative interpretation. It is non-indexical. Nothing outside the text is needed for interpretation. . . . In reading essayist prose the contextual clues to interpretation are in the text itself. (1981, 48)

They further maintain that this discourse system, which they call "essayist literacy," requires the "fictionalization of the audience and the author":

> The 'reader' of an essayist text is not an ordinary human being. It is an idealization, a rational mind formed by the rational body of knowledge of which the essay is a part. The reader is not allowed lapses of attention or idiosyncrasies. By the same token, the author is a fiction. The author as a person, by a process of writing and editing, seeks to achieve a state of self-effacement. (1981, 48–9)

In this modern consciousness, the writer and the reader ideally assume a stance of "solidarity politeness," a posture of intimacy and equipollence between reader and writer.

The Scollons conclude that "because learning to read and write in the essayist manner is in fact learning new patterns of discourse, literacy for the Athabaskan is experienced as a change of ethnicity as well as a change in reality set" (1981, 42). "[It is] only to the extent that [the Athabaskan] is modernized, has come to identify as an English speaker, that he or she can operate with the essayist ideal of literacy" (1981, 53).

The problems with the Scollons' work are manifold: while they seem to acknowledge that literacy is socially constituted, when they analyze "literacy" it changes from a human practice to a state of mind, a consciousness, or to a thing, an essayist text. With the construct of "essayist literacy" the Scollons brush away the social dynamics of reading and the fact that real readers are human beings. They, much like Ngũgĩ (see Chapter 2), construct a by-now familiar confabulation in which the language of the Other (here it is "essayist literacy") plays the role of arch-villain waving a deleterious wand on the cognition, and thus on community formations.

Because they believe that ethnicity is a thing, a commodity that should be preserved, the Scollons fail to see the dialectical implications inherent in the model of discourse processes that they appear to endorse (1981, 14). If the Athabaskans adopt the solidarity politeness of essayist literacy, they do not simply swap an Athabaskan identity for an English one. Instead, the Athabaskans engage in the "negotiation of intersubjective reality" that accompanies all discourse processes. They create a social world through ongoing negotiation. Discourse participants mutually present and alter their views of self and the world (1981, 14). The Athabaskans lose their "ethnic identity" as they and the Other become "more like each other" (1981, 201). In this interaction, the "we"/Other dynamic of ethnicity may dissolve, however temporarily, into a sense of universality. These ESL literacy practices provoke an awareness of ethnicity, followed by a negation of that instantiation of ethnicity and an awareness of plurality.

I do not mean to trivialize or denigrate the Scollons' overriding concern that differences in language and communicative styles are *somehow* associated with discrimination. I do dispute their account of how and why English literacy becomes the villain. Their argument is similar to that of Ngũgĩ. They claim that language differences are the source of discrimination against the Athabaskan natives. They fail to take account of the dialectics of language and social interaction, of ethnicity and universality, and of individual and social aspects of language acts. They blame language, pointing an accusatory finger at English literacy specifically. To make language the domineering protagonist in the story of discrimination is to obscure the economic and political relations that language mediates.

The ethnicists fail to see that when ESL writers or readers are conscious of "we" and an Other, this awareness is not always stable nor is it always negative, deleterious to participants in the literacy practices; this "we"/Other consciousness does not necessarily arise from imperious social interactions in which the Other dominates "me" so that "I" construct a "we" for protection.

The Vai of Liberia provide a provocative example because the tribe maintains literacy practices in three languages, Arabic, English, and Vai, although few individuals are tri-literate. In counterpoint to the ethnicist admonitions against ESL literacy, the Vai seem to use English literacy to preserve and protect their sense of community. In many instances English literacy practices are similar to Vai literacy practices. English is used for writing letters to friends, keeping family and business records, and maintaining diaries (Scribner and Cole, 85–6). Even when the mother tongue is suppressed, and English literacy practices mediate the "we"/Other dynamic, writing and reading are beneficial to the Vai. For example, Vai is prohibited as a language of written government communication. Those Vai who speak English "can act as buffers between the relatively powerful authorities in Monrovia and the relatively powerless rural inhabitants" (70). The Vai use written English to do government business and thus keep the Other out of the territory of everyday Vai life. These literacy practices actually help to maintain the separateness of the Vai community.

Whenever ESL literacy practices involve readers and writers in a "we"/Other relationship, a dynamic of universality is also immanent. Scribner and Cole claim that "the *world at large* can be found in the homes of English literate Vai people" (86, emphasis added). In fact, the "by no means trivial" difference between Vai and English literacy practices is that for the English literates "the world is reflected through the pages of *Time, Newsweek,* and the *Liberian Star*" (86). And the Vai do not seem to weaken their ties to their mother tongue communities as ESL literacy connects them with this "world at large." The Vai ESL literates may be drawn to opportunities in "modern occupations," in the "cash economy," but they are frequently disappointed with their ability to make a living and return to the farms and villages (64). It is not language but economics that motivates their migrations. For the Vai, English literacy practices do not necessarily carry the threat of ethnic dispersal; in fact, to the extent that ESL literacy engages the Vai in a "world at large," the engagement is characterized by abstract, symbolic relations rather than involvement with actual human beings and social institutions. Even when English literates do find employment in Monrovia or other large cities, they do not disperse throughout these cities but tend to live close to one another and maintain their cultural practices and community ties (86). Literacy does not generate the ability, or even necessarily the desire, to live in the world of the Other. The connections that ESL literacy fosters with a "world at large" do not concomitantly obliterate ties with the community of the mother tongue. Instead, ESL literacy practices facilitate a reconsideration of those ties and this reconsideration reformulates the community itself.

While the "we"/Other dynamic of ethnicity derives from difference, a sense of noncoincidence with the Other, universality results from ESL literates' desire for similarity or identity with the Other. However, the ESL literates' sense of identity with an Other, an abstract English speaking community, may be quixotic and ethereal. Our representations of self are recreated through our daily social interactions. If we are not interacting with the Other, if our sense of universality is based on our solitary reading of *Time* magazine, then the satisfaction of universality will be attenuated. The abstract nature of the dynamic of universality may, finally, propel ESL literates once again to seek out the earthly realities of the local, to create literacy practices concerned with one's family, friends, and coworkers, literacy practices intertwined with conversation, literacy practices which promote ethnicity.

ESL educators believe that ESL literacy is a neutral vehicle that promotes universality. They are not entirely wrong. It can promote the abstraction of universality. But they mistake abstract for neutral. And they fail to take into account the dialectical turn, the relations of ethnicity that are just around the corner, ever present.

Bakhtin and Vygotsky:
The Dialectics of Literacy and Social Relations

How does language, specifically text, mediate ethnicity and universality? Obviously literacy practices are not only social but also mental and individual. In what ways are the social and the individual mental aspects of literacy practices related? These questions are related to a larger issue—how is ESL literacy a social act? We know from Chapter 2 that many writers attribute social meanings to ESL reading and writing. They embrace or oppose and resist it on the basis of the social meanings they associate with ESL literacy practices, meanings derived from the social interactions which this literacy mediates. The work of Soviet language theorists Lev Vygotsky and M. M. Bakhtin are useful in thinking about these issues.

Vygotsky and Bakhtin begin their work with the premise that the individual and the social aspects of language are interdependent. They both believe that individual and private uses of language and literacy arise out of and retain the functions of social uses of language. Vygotsky, for example, argues that "the individual response emerges from the forms of collective life" (1981, 164–5). In their view, language, society, and culture are open and dynamic systems, capable of mutual influence, dialectical. And, in contrast to most Western linguists, who portray language as a reified thing, Bakhtin emphasizes the dynamic openness of language, its continual unfinishedness.

Because of the importance they put on language as social interaction, Vygotsky's and Bakhtin provide a point of departure for filling in details of the dialectics of ESL literacy practices; to call something a dialectic is to name it but is not necessarily to explain its processes. Applying many of Vygotsky and Bakhtin's principles to the problem of ESL literacy, we can explore the dialectics.

Vygotsky's work points to the following question: How does language mediate social interaction and thought? In Vygotskian theory, social interaction is characterized as an "interpsychological process" that signs, and language in particular, mediate. These interpsychological processes are not, however, an aspect of the psychology of an individual; rather they are concrete social interactions involving small groups or dyads of individuals. In describing the social origins of "higher mental functions" (also referred to as processes of "cultural development"), Vygotsky suggests that "interpsychological processes" are internalized, creating "intrapsychological processes." Through this internalization, "outer speech" becomes "inner speech." In this fashion, the psychological and the social are inextricably intertwined. Vygotsky articulates the relationship between the mental and the social relations of language and thought that the Scollons found so difficult to explain. The social is not a factor or a stimulus contributing to psychological processes. Instead, psychological processes are viewed as genetically social.

The process of internalization was the primary object of analysis for Vygotsky:

> The very mechanism underlying higher mental function is a copy from social interaction; all higher mental functions are internalized social relationships. . . . Their composition, genetic structure, and means of action [forms of mediation]—in a word, their whole nature—is social. Even when we turn to mental [internal] processes, their nature remains quasi-social. In their own private sphere, human beings retain the functions of social interaction. (1981, 164)

Vygotsky also suggests that intrapsychological processes are not completely isomorphic with interpsychological processes. In fact, Vygotsky states that the "internalization of [interpsychological processes] transforms the process itself and changes its structure and functions" (1981, 163). The mental is not a copy of the social, not completely determined by the social.

Vygotsky's ideas help to explain how ethnicity and universality are immanent in each other. Every literacy practice has an internal and an external dimension. As these practices are internalized, by definition they may involve far less direct contact with Others, but social interaction is represented in the writers' and readers' heads. In this representation, the reader/writer may create imaginary worlds in which the boundaries between "we" and Other are recast, over and over. In this sense, the social relations of ethnicity are precursors to the mental abstractions of universality. Ethnicity is lived and represented; universality emerges as a secondary representation of ethnicity. In other words, universality represents, in different form (literally re-presenting), the social relations of ethnicity.

As ESL writers/readers try on alternative identities, shadow dancing with the Other, they are also reconceiving their literacy practices—who they read and write for and with. They may, in turn, remake the actual social construction of their literacy practices. This is not to say that ESL writers can imagine away the material realities of social and economic boundaries. Clearly they cannot. Nor does it mean, as Richard Rodríguez would argue, that ESL literacy will create more and better social relations with the Other, and this in turn will redistribute money, jobs, and power. Clearly, ESL literacy will not. But this dialectic does make it possible for ESL writers to move beyond dichotomies, to think dialectically, to imagine polyphonic cultures, new identities, multivoiced texts which help to create new social spaces in which these writers can live.

It is not only Vygotsky who believed thought (inner speech) and conversation (outer speech) to be related in structure and function. Bakhtin describes inner speech as a "dialogue between two voices." Bakhtin further argues that

> the units of which inner speech is constituted . . . resemble the alternating lines of a dialogue. There was good reason why thinkers in ancient times should have conceived of inner speech as inner dialogue. . . . Only by ascertaining the forms of whole utterances and, especially, the forms of dialogic speech, can light be shed on the forms of inner speech as well as on the peculiar logic of their concatenation in the stream of speech. (Voloshinov 1973, 38)

In the individual there are many voices, many languages, many selves. The self is not totally determined by the social dynamics of a dyad, group, or institution. Or, as Caryl Emerson points out:

> In the Bakhtinian model, every individual engages in two perpendicular activities. He forms lateral ("horizontal") relationships with

other individuals in specific speech acts, and he simultaneously forms internal ("vertical") relationships between the outer world and his own psyche. These double activities are constant, and their interactions in fact constitute the psyche. The psyche is not an internal but a boundary phenomenon. (1983, 249)

Or, in Bakhtin's own words:

Language, for the individual consciousness, lies on the borderline between oneself and the other. The word in language is half some-one else's. (1981, 294)

Vygotsky's interpsychological and intrapsychological processes parallel Bakhtin's "horizontal" and "vertical" relationships respectively and these correspondences help to further elaborate the dialectics of ethnicity and universality.

While Vygotsky focuses on the social and mental processes mediated by a sign system, Bakhtin analyzes language, the sign system itself. He believes that all language is heteroglossic, dialogic, awhirl in the push and pull of centripedal and centrifugal forces which unify and diversify it simultaneously, continually. ESL writers' language is rich in a struggle between the language of "we," the mother tongue(s), and the language of the Other, English. In the heteroglossia of ESL literacy we find the dialectic of ethnicity and universality. (See Chapter 6 for an elaboration of the pedagogical implications of this point.)

Bakhtin's discussion of "authoritative discourse" is a starting point for rethinking the relationships between second language acquisition and ESL literacy practices. "The authoritative word is located in a distanced zone, we encounter it with its authority already fused to it" (1981, 342):

It is not a free appropriation and assimilation of the word itself that authoritative discourse seeks to elicit from us; rather, it demands our unconditional allegiance. Therefore authoritative discourse permits no play with the context framing it, no play with its borders, no gradual and flexible transitions, no spontaneously creative stylizing variants on it. . . . It is indissolubly fused with its authority— with political power, an institution, a person . . . a playing with distances, with fusion and dissolution, with approach and retreat, is not here possible. (1981, 344)

For most teachers, the goal of ESL literacy education is not, in the case of English, to "play with its borders."[1] It is not to create "stylizing variants" of English. It is, in Bakhtin's words, to "assimilate another's discourse."[2] Accordingly, the discourse of the ESL literacy class is for the most part authoritative. While ESL teachers recognize that their students' interlanguage is systematic, necessary, and evidence of language acquisition, they do not and cannot find it to be virtuous English. Almost without exception, the ESL teacher assumes that students will and should learn to speak and write standard English, a construct which assumes that a language is forever finished with definite borders, a unified entity. What gives standard English these definite (albeit fictional) margins is the political power of those drawing the dividing lines. In Bakhtin's words, authoritative discourse is "fused" to "political power." It is hardly surprising that the authoritative discourse promoted by ESL teachers can inaugurate and/or perpetuate a dynamic of ethnicity in which the student rejects the word and opposes the Other.

There is an alternative. While English may come to the student indelibly fused to authority, the teacher may challenge that union. The teacher can expose the fiction, questioning the reality of a monolithic word. The teacher can present a view of language as heteroglossic rather than absolute and pure. She can talk of language acquisition as appropriation. As Bakhtin suggests, one can appropriate the word of the Other, even if this word is authoritative, and use it to form one's own discourse. In this process the word becomes "internally persuasive." The teacher can encourage students to resist the authoritative pull and confront the language of the Other through appropriation. The word, and often the social relations which are thereby mediated, can be reshaped; they are literally re-presented. Conversely, the word can be appropriated only when the social relations constituting it are no longer authoritative.

This internally persuasive ESL discourse neither imitates nor reproduces the authority of native speakers. It is neither deaf nor closed to other languages and cultures. On the boundary line between cultures and languages, English struggles with other discourses. This writing/reading of ESL students is "interanimated."

As it turns out, neither the ethnicists nor the universalists had the whole story wrong. They just didn't have the whole story. ESL literacy may bring with it imperious social relations and authoritative discourse. If ESL students reject this discourse, then obviously there is no development, no language acquisition or appropriation, no forging of new forms of language and culture. If, however, a student's opposition can become playful resistance, a pushing back, then development may occur in the interanimation of the word. This pushing back happens as the ESL writer appropriates the word. Literacy development occurs through the continual movement of the dialectic, not when the ESL writer/reader moves unidirectionally from ethnicity to universality, or when the ESL writer settles on some permanent mix of the two.

Resistance involves the ESL writer in dialogue, in multiple voices, with multiple readerships. The appropriation of which

Bakhtin speaks becomes an analogue of resistance, and this is what constitutes ESL literacy development. Ethnicity becomes more than opposition to ESL literacy practices; it turns to resist the ways in which these literacy practices may control (through the social relations that they mediate). The ESL writer defies not only a reified English but also a sense of permanent reified difference.

For ESL teachers to encourage this type of resistance would require dismantling deep-seated habits of mind and systems of authenticity. This would also lead to a redefinition of language acquisition that does not privilege a student's mimicking the standard language. It would require teachers to deliberately challenge the fiction of a unified and stable standard language. It would instead encourage students and teachers alike "to play with distances, with fusion and dissolution, with approach and retreat." It would ask teachers to redefine their sense of a universal language, from neutral Adamic purity to full blown heteroglossia.

On the boundaries of Babel, we recast the word and we question the worlds that it mediates.

Notes

1. There are, of course, exceptions. Of note is Brownyn Norton Peirce's "Pedagogy of Possibility" in South Africa.

2. Of interest here is Lynn Goldstein's research on ESL students' acquisition of non-standard English.

Chapter Four

"America Is in the Heart": ESL Literacy and Everyday Life

America Is in the Heart ([1943] 1973) is the autobiography of Carlos Bulosan, a writer who came to the United States in 1930 from his home village of Binaloan in the Philippines. At seventeen, with three years of formal schooling and little knowledge of English, Bulosan arrived on the West Coast. He was typical of the many young unmarried Filipinos who came to the United States between 1907 and 1930 to settle in California and work in farm labor camps.

Bulosan's story both narrates and constitutes his departure from and subsequent return to the limits and severity of village life in the Philippines. Literacy practices mediated Bulosan's relationships with his "roots," his native land and family, and his relationship to America and Americans. His story exemplifies the theoretical description of ESL literacy put forth in Chapter 3. Bulosan's text also enacts the meaning which he attributes to literacy in English; in other words, *America Is in the Heart* is a self-reflexive text, not only representing Bulosan's engagement in literacy practices but demonstrating them.

In his autobiography, Bulosan affords little mention of the fact that he writes in a second language, English. Bulosan as autobiographer appears totally untutored in the ideology that the soul of a people is embodied in their mother tongue. With this linguistic nonchalance, his story contrasts sharply with those of the ethnicists and the universalists who describe an English which is either monstrous or liberatory. Rather than focus on language per se, Bulosan's tale centers on his social interactions with both Filipinos and Americans, relationships in which and through which reading and writing in English became increasingly important.

Bulosan's tale is not a bucolic hymn to the pleasures and virtues of life and literacy in democratic America. In fact, Carey McWilliams introduces the text with the statement that "America Is in the Heart is a deeply moving account of what it is like to be treated as a criminal in a strange and alien society" ([1943] 1973, vii). The text is packed with reversals in which Bulosan continually reformulates his relations to and definitions of Filipino and American cultures and communities. ESL literacy practices are both juxtaposed with and generative of physical violence. Importantly, they become the arena through which Bulosan is able to both control and assimilate the Other.

The dialectic of ethnicity and universalism manifests itself in both the events narrated and the language and form of the narration. In my analysis of America Is in the Heart, I assume that the events are Bulosan's representation of what Vygotsky calls interpsychological processes, while the language and form of the narration represent intrapsychological processes.

Childhood

"The predatory years," is the epithet that Bulosan uses for his childhood and early adolescence, described in the first third of the text. This is the story of the dissolution of his family as they struggled with poverty and illness. Everyday life was punctuated with the deaths and births of children and the marriages of his older brothers. His eldest brother, Macario, was the son chosen to be educated. But the cost of Macario's education in a nearby town meant that those Bulosans left behind ate less, fewer fish and more rice. As time went on Macario's schooling meant increasing sacrifices: family land had to be sold and even rice had to be eaten sparingly. The family dreamed that Macario would eventually return to the barrio and teach, helping to support the ever enlarging Bulosan family. Briefly this dream materialized when Macario did return for a short time. Soon after, however, he left for the utopian United States.

Carlos himself eventually left the farm. First he went to a nearby town, joining his mother who lived there, bartering salted fish for beans and rice. Later he sought employment in the small cities yet farther away from the paternal lands. Bulosan describes himself as shoeless, with shoulder length hair "tangled like a bird's nest" during this period of his life. Yet he managed to attend school sporadically, in between bouts of illness and near starvation.

Within this Cimmerian atmosphere, Bulosan associates literacy practices with "the beginning of understanding," "an emerging into sunlight" (71). Literacy did not, however, become significant for Bulosan in the usual institutional context of education. He did not develop literacy values in school. Instead, he learned that reading and writing had value through interactions with two elder brothers, a friend, and an American librarian. Bulosan suggests not only that literacy became important through social relationships, but also the corollary, that these relationships became significant because they were connected to reading.

His elder brother Macario, for example, read him various tales of salvation: first, the story of Robinson Crusoe in which Macario "patiently explained the struggle of this ingenious man who had lived alone for years in inclement weather and had survived loneliness and returned safely to his native land" (32). Bulosan could not decode the words of the story by himself, but he repeated aloud the line that Macario intoned, instructing him "to remember the good example of Robinson Crusoe." This incident, Bulosan says, "marked the beginning of my intellectual life with Macario, the beginning of sharing our thoughts with each other" (32). Macario also read to Bulosan from the Old Testament, the story of "Moses who delivered his persecuted people to safety in another land." Bulosan says that these interactions "filled me with wonder as [Macario] explained the significance of the great men who had died for their persecuted peoples centuries ago" (45).

These narratives from Bulosan's early childhood were the texts which began his intellectual life; they provided the text that Bulosan would reproduce to explain the struggles of his own life. Bulosan represents his own life story as an analogue to those of Robinson Crusoe and Moses: he journeyed to a remote, foreign place where he would work to liberate himself and his people, the Filipino peasants, from oppression.

In the early pages of America Is in the Heart, Bulosan associates literacy practices with perspicacity, liberation, flight, and "travel through history into other lands and times" (46). Some of these escapes which Bulosan imagines are symbolic, others not. An American librarian employs Bulosan as a houseboy. Then she realizes that he has an interest in reading and arranges for him to work in the library. There he found "great pleasure," not in reading or being read to, but in "be[ing] close to books," in dusting them, touching them, and delivering them to middle-class homes (70–1). While searching for a way out of poverty, for alternatives to daily destitution, he encounters people who encourage him to leave the Philippines. A Filipino houseboy reads to Bulosan about Abraham Lincoln, "A poor boy [who] became president of the United States!" (69). What the houseboy implies is that literacy enabled Lincoln to escape poverty. This friend encourages Bulosan to learn English because it is a "weapon" through which one can flee the destitution of everyday life as a Filipino peasant. Bulosan suggests that his route away from the poverty of the Philippines was symbolically facilitated by his interactions with this librarian and houseboy, interactions that were mediated by ESL literacy practices.

Additionally, his elder brother, Luciano, instructs him in the value of literacy:

> You must never stop reading good books. . . . [G]o to Manila someday and buy a pair of good glasses. . . . Reading is food for the mind. Healthy ideas are food for the mind. Maybe someday you will be a journalist. (56)

Interestingly, for Luciano, and by implication for Bulosan, literacy is hardly ethereal. Literacy practices are intimately connected to the body: to eyeglasses, and metaphorically, to nutrition. Literacy also gives substance to a dream of better employment, a change of social class even, in the future.

Luciano's advice and the stories that were read to Bulosan were sources of the meanings that he would assign to literacy practices. Throughout *America Is in the Heart*, Bulosan connects literacy with escape from a mental and material, inchoate and moribund, darkness which he describes as the "narrowness of the world" (238). Literacy practices, he repeatedly claims, gave him a vision of a "universal brotherhood," fraternal relationships that worked together to constitute a sanguine and democratic society. This value for literacy was not contingent upon his own decoding of an encoding of texts but was built from the content of the stories read to him, tales of Robinson Crusoe's isolation and return to his native land, Abraham Lincoln's rise from poverty to presidency, and Moses' leading his people to freedom. Each of these stories provided him with a model for living and for telling stories about his life.

This early advice of Luciano's stays with Bulosan. Many years later Bulosan comes to believe that he can recuperate his own history through writing:

> Years afterward I remembered Luciano's hope. . . . And far away also, in the workers' republic of Spain, a civil war was going on that a democracy might live. I remembered all my years in the

Philippines my father fighting for his inherited land, my mother selling boggoong to the impoverished peasants. I remembered all my brothers and their bitter fight for a place in the sun, their tragic fear that they might not live long enough to contribute something vital to the world. I remembered my own swift and dangerous life in America. And I cried, recalling all the years that had come and gone, but my remembrance gave me a strange courage and the vision of a better life.

Yes, I will be a writer and make all of you live again in my words, I sobbed. (56–7)

The United States: The Migrant Years

"The years of the great hatred," the years after Bulosan moved to the United States, are the subject of the second third of the text (143). In this portion of the narrative Bulosan represents America and the Americans as alien, a radical Other. Both literally and figuratively, Bulosan does not know where to locate himself in the foreign world of America. He travels by freight train, moving often up and down the coast, through seasons and places identified by the names of fruits and vegetables. Grapes. Lettuce. Linguistically, he places himself outside of the community of Filipino farm workers. He writes about "the Filipino." He repudiates the "desperate cynicism" he sees in their lives saturated with economic and sexual exploitation, alcohol and violence (132).

However, eventually social boundaries of "we" and Other change. Bulosan acquires gambling skills that become his entree into "their" world. He comes to identify with the Filipino workers. He stands in opposition to the Americans, saying: "I knew that our decadence was imposed by a society alien to our character and inclination, alien to our heritage and history" (135).

This "we"/Other dynamic became conscious and articulated through social interactions mediated by literacy. Two examples are particularly salient. First, Bulosan's brother Macario introduced him to a Filipino writer. This author claims that he will not have been "a writer in America in vain" because he will "write a great book about the Ilocano peasants in northern Luzon" (139). Bulosan carries one of this writer's stories with him and interprets the inter-action as follows, "Thus it was that I began to rediscover my native land and the cultural roots there that had nourished me, and I felt a great urge to identify myself with the social awakening of my people" (139). And, later, Bulosan is compelled to write a letter to his brother Macario because he realizes that he feels compassion rather than disgust for the "workers in the field":

Then it actually came to me, like a revelation, that I could actually write understandable English. I was seized with happiness. I wrote slowly and boldly, drinking the wine when I stopped, laughing silently and crying. When the long letter was finished, a letter which was actually a story of my life, I jumped to my feet and shouted through my tears: "They can't silence me any more! I'll tell the world what they have done to me!" (180)

By writing and reading in English, Bulosan finds and articulates his connections to the Filipino community. It is no longer the Filipinos who are "they" but the Americans. Writing has enabled him to represent his social interactions with his fellow farm laborers in everyday life.

When Bulosan does write, "I" is not his topic nor is "the world" his audience. From Pascual, a Filipino lawyer, and his brother Macario, Bulosan learns that a Filipino should write to and for his own community; literacy should be catalytic to the formation of Filipino community and culture. The lawyer, a man whose "talent had found fuller expression in writing," had started a newspaper for the farm workers in Stockton, California. He instructs Bulosan that "it is for the workers that we must write. . . . [W]e must interpret their hopes as a people desiring the fullest fulfillment of their potentialities." The newspaper was not long lived. As Bulosan's literacy practices changed, so did his social relationships. Each affected the other in the dialectical whirlwind in which the lines of cause and effect are always a bit blurry. Bulosan comments that "[Pascual] belonged to yesterday" (187).

Macario, who had started a literary magazine with a group of friends provides Bulosan with an alternative vision, one that he seems to find preferable to the "we"/Other dynamic preferred by Pascual. In a long speech that Bulosan as narrator claims to be able to reproduce verbatim, Macario says:

It has fallen upon us to inspire a united front among our people. . . . We must achieve articulation of social ideas, not only for some kind of economic security, but also to help culture bloom as it should in our time. We are approaching what will be the greatest achievement of our generation: the discovery of a new vista of literature, that is, to speak to the people and to be understood by them. (188)

Bulosan, as narrator and as implied author, Macario, and Pascual share the belief that writing should create a "people" and culture. They propose, then, an ideology of ethnicity.

Nothing dialectical is ever so stable and clear as the doctrine of ethnicity appears in the first part of Macario's speech. Later in the same speech, the dialectical tension between ethnicity and

universality becomes apparent. The "we" of ethnicity is an artifact
of ongoing social processes; ethnicity is a mutable relation mediated
by language that creates an illusion of stability and simultaneously
reveals its instability. In discourse, the pronoun *we*, for example,
only appears to have a stable referent. While this pronoun may appear throughout a discourse, the referent may subtly shift, including
or excluding, constantly redefining who the Other is. In Macario's
speech, the relationship of "we" to "them" becomes "We are [them]."
As he pronounces "We are America. . . . [T]he old world is dying, but
a new world is being born," (187) he is not promoting assimilation
but a construction of America as a global community.

   The dialectical simultaneity of ethnicity and universality is apparent in Bulosan's own literacy practices. He meets several American writers and editors who encourage him to write by telling him
that he will be a "great American poet." But, while voraciously reading American poets, Bulosan himself envisions the trajectory of his
writing to move through and ultimately beyond an American identity. He describes this dialectical movement as follows:

> I could follow the path of these poets, continue their tradition, and
> if, at the end of my career, I could arrive at a positive understanding
> of America, then I could go back to the Philippines with a torch of
> enlightenment. (228)

As Bulosan's story continues, his reading and writing take on new
meanings through these social interactions. In turn, these interactions take on new meanings through reading and writing.

   Bulosan describes his relationship with a woman named Eileen,
and in this story we find a rich source of detail about the process
through which social interaction mediated by literacy leads to appropriation of English:

> But she talked but little when she came to see me. When she left,
> leaving some books, I imagined I read the words she would have
> spoken. . . . We found intimate conversations in the books she gave
> me. When I became restless, I wrote to her. Every day the words
> poured out of my pen. I began to cultivate a taste for words, not so
> much their meanings as the sounds and shapes, so that afterward I
> tried to depend on the music of words to express my ideas. This
> procedure, of course, was destructive to my grammar, but I can say
> that writing fumbling vehement letters to Eileen was actually my
> course in English. (234–5)

Bulosan finds books through Eileen, and he constructs Eileen
through books. As Bulosan describes it, "I created for myself an
illusion of understanding with Eileen." (234–5). This relationship
itself invites, nearly seduces, him to appropriate English. He hears

music in the Other language. He goes farther; he uses this music to create ideas. But, not surprisingly, Bulosan's music destroyed his shaky control of and grounding in standard English. Pushing on a reified English, a "grammar," he discovered polyphony.

Through his literacy with Eileen, America becomes the land of the universal for Bulosan. He "yearn[s] for . . . the world she represented. . . . I told her these things in poems" (234). Eileen was "the America I had wanted to find. . . . This America was human and good and real" (236).

To reiterate, Bulosan did not have an "integrative motivation" for writing or for learning English, to use the terms of social psychologists Gardner and Lambert. He was not concerned with assimilation. He was drawn to social interactions that took place through the symbolic actions of reading and writing. He was deeply moved by the inter- and intrapsychological processes that interdependently create the community, both symbolic and material, that he is calling "America."

When Bulosan becomes so ill that he must be hospitalized, he reads to continue his search for community, for "roots," but "community" evolves once again into a utopian universal. At the time of his physical isolation, he loses even the hope for a material, local community. He writes that "it is much easier for us who have no roots to integrate ourselves in a universal ideal—that there are men of goodwill all over the world, in every race, in all classes" (241). His universal ideal is first shaped while reading "Rilke, Kafka, Lorca, writers [who] collectively represented a heroism of the spirit . . . so gloriously had they succeeded in inspiring a universal brotherhood among men" (238). In his isolation, Bulosan's universal community becomes increasingly abstract:

> So from day to day, I read and reading widened my mental horizon, creating a spiritual kinship with other men who had pondered over the miseries of their countries. Place did not matter. . . . I plunged into books, boring through the earth's core, leveling all seas and oceans, swimming in the constellations. (246)

Bulosan's immersion in reading began along with real people, his brother and Eileen, but developed through a relationship he created with foreign poets and novelists, who in turn evolved into a "universal brotherhood." Bulosan finishes this strain of his literacy practices without people, either real or symbolic. His immersion in books separated him from the other patients in the hospital. He blames reading for causing him to feel "lost and lonely." Mentally, he dwells not with heroes or representations of people, but in the stars, the seas, and the "earth's core."

Bulosan is unsatisfied living in this universal world, a universe no longer grounded in, no longer a representation stemming from, actual social interaction. It is a second order abstraction. This is the ideology of the universal. Its potential to slip out of the actual material world of social interaction and reside in the abstract— the heroes of afar or even in the stars—generates its dialectical tension.

Once outside the hospital, Bulosan involves himself with the Communist Party, the CIO, and the Committee for the Protection of Filipino Rights. He writes newspaper articles and pamphlets. He reads. This time, however, he returns to "the folklore of my own country, the heroes and the tales of the Philippines. He searches for other Asian writers writing in English, and he finds satisfaction in the works of Yonehill Kang and Yone Noguchi" (256).

To his writing he once again ascribes the purposes of community formation. This time he wants a community limited to Filipinos: "I sat at the bare table in the kitchen and began piecing together the mosaic of our lives in America. Full of loneliness and love, I began to write" (289, emphasis added). By the end of the text, Bulosan seems to have come to terms with literacy and with America and with the relationship between the two. He continues to anchor his reading and writing in the interactions that represent and create community. "America," he says, "is ours" (324).

Bulosan juxtaposes literacy and violence, and in so doing most dramatically announces the significance he attributes to literacy practices. Back and forth, he accepts the fist fights and the beatings, and then he repudiates them. Toward the violence endemic in the farm- and factory-worker Filipino communities, he is alternatively attracted and repulsed. For a time, he heeds the advice of a newspaper editor who encourages him to be an aggressor with words rather than with guns. Ultimately, however, Bulosan finds but hollowness in the editor's exhortations to "write your guts out! write with thunder and blood!" (183). Poignantly he explains his dilemma:

> I was intellectually stimulated again—and I wanted to discuss problems which had been bothering me. But when I came home to our apartment, sitting alone in the midst of drab walls and ugly furniture, I felt like striking at my invisible foe. Then I began to write. (305)

Bulosan places great hope in the act of writing:

> The time had come, I felt, for me to utilize my experience in written form. I had something to live for now, and to fight the world with; and I was no longer afraid of the past. I felt that I would not run away from myself again. (306)

Bulosan euphoniously describes the powers of literacy, but his belief in literacy's force disintegrates as he copes with "the impossiblity of finding a decent house" (306). It is, in fact, the exigencies and the violence of his day-to-day existence that drive him to acknowledge the false promises of literacy. "I sensed the futility of writing. I wanted action—and violence" (308). What Bulosan finds, however, is temporary solace in an alcoholic stupor. He "wander[s] aimlessly in Golden Gate Park," and the friend who finds him in this state encourages him to return to literacy. Promoting the ideology of ethnicity, the friend tells Bulosan that he can find salvation by writing the stories of his childhood. Bulosan, however, is no longer vulnerable to the promises of community found in and through ethnic literacy. His response is ominous: "I have tried [writing] several times. If I fail again, I could become the most vicious Filipino criminal in America" (309).

By the end of the narrative, however, Bulosan has published a small book of poetry, *Letters from America*, the title connoting his symbolic return, through literacy, to the Philippines. Bulosan has finally embraced the America he has been able to create through social interactions mediated by his literacy practices.

The Dialectics of Language

In *America Is in the Heart* the dialectic of ethnicity and universality is enacted not only through the events which Bulosan narrates, but also through his language. Bulosan's construction of the Other and the "we," his relations to Filipino communities and Americans are continually shifting. The changes in these relationships are registered in the voice images of the text. Through these voices, Bulosan constructs the selves that he will be through his social relations and his representation of them. As Bakhtin writes, linguistic structures are ideologically rich; "the word is the most sensitive index of social changes" (Volosinov 1973, 19).

Stylistically the first third of *America Is in the Heart* is characterized by an interweaving of three narrative "voices" (Bakhtin 1981, 262), three "compositional-stylistic unities," each associated with Bulosan as narrator, each constructing an ideological position. These positions are composed in the dialogic relations among the voices. These dialogic relations will be referred to as dialogue even though these voices do not belong to separate characters who address each other in conversation. The narrator has several voices, engaging in various conversations with the others throughout the text. The first voice presents a "direct authorial literary-artistic narration" of events. The second consists of "various forms of literary but extra-artistic authorial speech (moral, philosophical or scientific statements, oratory, ethnographic description, memoranda, and so forth)" (Bakhtin 1981, 262). This second voice speaks as an historian or an ethnographer; it is an essayist voice that comments on the social situation in which the narrative is taking place. The third voice could be described as a combination of the two. At the beginnings and endings of chapters, this voice instructs the reader how to interpret the events of the narrative, on how and why these events are significant and related to the whole of Bulosan's life; this voice speaks from the future about the past; it interprets events (ongoing within the narrative structure) in terms of future ones. Unlike the "hybrid constructions" that Bakhtin identifies in the novels that he calls polyphonic, these voices are fairly clearly demarcated. They occur in separate sentences and even in distinct paragraph units. They do not generally cross sentence boundaries.

In dialogue, the voices assert the "we" and the Other of ethnicity. The Other is put forth first, and slowly the "we" evolves out of the dialogue between the historian voice and the narrator voice. The historian points out that "they" and "them" are responsible for the poverty and social upheaval in the Philippines:

> The Philippines was undergoing a radical social change; all over the archipelago the younger generation was stirring and adapting new attitudes. . . . For a time it seemed that the younger generation, influenced by false American ideals and modes of living, had become total strangers to the older generation. In the provinces where the poor peasants lived and toiled for the rich haciendaros, or landlords, the young men were stirring and rebelling against their heritage. (5)

By itself this voice does not call forth the dynamics of ethnicity. This voice argues that the Americans are the Other, but so are the Filipinos. There is no reference to a "we." This essayist voice speaks of both the peasants and the foreigners in the third person. This voice tells of the struggles of the peasants against the Spanish but does not align itself with either group:

> One summer day, when the rice lay golden in the sun, startling rumors came to Mangusmana: the peasants in the province to the south of us had revolted against their landlords. There the peasants had been the victims of ruthless exploitation for years, dating back to the eighteenth century when Spanish colonizers instituted severe restrictive measures in order to impoverish the native. . . . The peasants did not know to whom they should present their grievances or whom to fight when the cancer of exploitation became intolerable. They became cynical about the national government and the few

powerful Filipinos of foreign extraction who were squeezing a fat
livelihood out of it. (23)

The narrator of ongoing events speaks of "I" and "my brother" and
third person relationships: "he," "they," and so forth. This voice
asserts an individualist subject. Referring to "the peasants" in the
third person, this voice excludes himself and his family from the
peasant class, claiming that "many of the peasants were starving, but
like my family they were full of pride" (36).

The retrospective narrator transforms this "I"/"they" relation
(they indicating the Filipino peasants). The narrator suggests the
possibility of the subject's community with the peasants:

> I knelt on the wet cement picking out the dirt and pebbles from the
> beans. It was another discovery: my first clash with the middle
> classes in the Philippines. Afterward I came to know their social
> attitude, their stand on the peasant problem. I knew where they
> stood regarding national issues. I hated their arrogance and their
> contempt for the peasantry. . . . I was one peasant who did not crawl
> on my knees and say: "It is all right. It is all right." (38)

The retrospective narrator changes the subject position. Suddenly
"they" refers not to the peasants, but to the middle class. In the middle
of the paragraph, with the phrase "I was one peasant, " Bulosan begins to speak from the subject position of the peasant, but he maintains the single subject "I" in relation to this class. He does not belong
to the "we," but the dialogue among the voices has created a "we" of
the Filipino peasants even though Bulosan is ambivalent about his
relation to this community.

Bulosan speaks in many voices, many selves as he defines and
redefines himself, the Other, and the relationship between the two.
In concert, these voices assert a "we"/Other relationship between the
Filipino peasantry and the middle class of foreign extraction,
whether Spanish or American.

Interestingly Americans and the English language are not implicated in the ideology of ethnicity. Rather, Americans become associated with the doctrine of universality through their connection to
education in the Philippines. The historian voice praises the Americans and their "free" and "popular" education that was "spreading
throughout the archipelago and open[ing] new opportunities" (14).
The narrator celebrates this education, claiming that it "brought a
new and democratic system . . . into the Philippines." Education
awoke "a nation hitherto illiterate and backward" (14). "Contact with
American ideals was actually the liberation of their potentialities as
a people and the discovery of the natural wealth of their land" (47).
The historian voice further explains that prior to the United States'

involvement, education was restricted to "rulers" and a few middle class Filipinos "who could manage to go to Europe" (14). Even the Other, in this case the "Mohammedan Moors," would benefit from an American education, the narrator proclaims.

This historian narrator voice also implies that education is incendiary, leading to often violent action against social injustices:

> In every house and hut in the far-flung barrios where the common man or tao was dehumanized by absentee landlordism, where a peasant had a son who went to school through the sacrifice of his family and who came back with invigorating ideas of social equality and of equal justice before the law, there grew a great conflict that threatened to plunge the Philippines into one of its bloodiest revolutions. (24)

Bulosan represents his own history here. His brother Macario, was, in fact, "a son who went to school through the sacrifice of his family."

This tale of a "free" and "popular" education ruptures. This perspective on education, on the Americans, and their affiliation with the doctrine of universality is contested by Bulosan's own narrative. Echoes of Bulosan's own sacrifices for Macario disrupt the totality of this voice and its romantic mythology of education and Americans. The sacrifices of the "predatory years" haunt the text, which as a whole indirectly denies the assertion that education, particularly American education, is the key to salvation.

The text may not place Americans within the "we"/Other relations of ethnicity, but neither does it unequivocally associate them with the doctrine of universality and the negation of the "we"/Other dynamic. If anything, it is literacy practices that are most intimately linked to an abolition of the "we"/Other relation even though these literacy practices occur in English, a foreign language. (See also in Chapter 3 the discussion of the Vai.) Perhaps because Americans were not central to the dynamic of ethnicity at this point in the text, literacy could be the force through which an ideology of universality could emerge. The fact that these literacy practices were in English was incidental. The oppression was carried out by the Spanish, so no one viewed English or ESL literacy as treacherous to Filipino native culture.

When Bulosan writes about his move to the United States, his relationship to Americans changes. As the literacy practices which Bulosan describes reveal an ideology of ethnicity so do the voices or voice of the text. Americans do become the Other; Bulosan creates a Filipino "we" of which he is a part. This Other and this community are in dialectical relation to the drive for universality. The narrative voice takes over and dominates the text; put in other terms, the interpsychological processes that are described in and the intrapsychological processes that are revealed by the text are more or less isomorphic.

Bulosan's story demonstrates the social dimensions of ESL literacy practices. Literacy practices both develop social interaction and develop through social interaction. Literacy practices mediate relations with the "Other." After hearing Bulosan's story, it is difficult to imagine writing and reading as "thinking processes" primarily, or as activities that are about language acquisition centrally.

The social relations that literacy mediates, however, are not always liberatory. Literacy practices facilitate oppression as well as freedom. Throughout his life Bulosan struggled to relate to the Other. Sometimes he chose literacy; at others, he chose fists and guns.

Chapter Five

ESL Literacy, Communitas, and Classroom Practices

If ESL literacy practices are social acts, what and how do we teach? What are the goals of the ESL literacy class? If ESL literacy practices involve writers and readers in dynamics of identity and difference, a dialectic of ethnicity and universality that is evident in both inter- and intrapsychological processes, what does this mean for the ESL class? How can this theoretical insight be used to shape and guide educational practices?

In answering these questions, I also want to challenge the traditional dichotomy of "the real world" and education. I want to question the idea that education is a process, not only segregated from, but also subordinate to the real world, the idea that education cannot change or influence society but can only service or ignore its dictates. The English language class is part of the social world in which literacy practices are constituted. From this perspective, the function of the ESL literacy course is not to conform to the dictates of a hypothetical "real" world but to contribute to its social formations. Put in different terms, the ways in which ESL literacy is learned, the literacy practices of the classroom, are what constitute the meaning of ESL literacy for many students. There is not a better or purer literacy in the world outside the class; ESL literacy is what students' experience tells them it is. For students who experience literacy only or primarily through the social interaction of schooling, what literacy *is* often depends on how it is taught and learned.

The ESL literacy class should be seen as a whole in which the processes of social interaction, language acquisition (redefined as language appropriation), and reading and writing are dialectically related. If acquisition of standard English is seen as the privileged goal of the class, as is often the case, writing or composing is likely to be perceived by student and teacher alike as a practice activity as a "language exercise" rather than as a "social activity" (Widdowson 1983, 44). And, as a study by Ann Raimes suggests, students "who view the task as one of negotiation with a reader [may] ultimately make more progress in their writing than those who see the task solely as a linguistic problem" (1985, 251). Placing language acquisition at the center of the ESL literacy class does not result in the production of native-like writers and readers. Privileging language acquisition may suppress literacy because students fear, avoid, and reject writing and reading in a language they cannot quite "get right." They may see literacy as an exercise, a hoop through which to jump, over and over again. Writing native-like prose is too restrictive a goal for ESL literacy pedagogy. Reading and writing classes for nonnative speakers should explore and enhance the social purposes and relations which mediate ESL literacy practices. When the social is enriched, the language will be too.

Communitas

In an attempt to find a root metaphor that can guide educational practice in ESL literacy, a metaphor to counter that of Babel, I look to the work of anthropologist Victor Turner. Turner is of particular interest because he analyzes the relationship of marginals, outsiders, and liminars to social processes and social structures. Turner is especially interested in the dialectical relationship of social structure and what he calls anti-structure—the processes, actions, and interactions that undermine the structures of everyday life. Turner's construct of *communitas* helps to explain how the dialectics of ethnicity and universality could play themselves out productively in the ESL literacy class.

Most ESL literacy students are what Turner would call marginals. To greater and lesser degrees, they live everyday life outside of the mainstream, native speaking culture. Permanently or temporarily, they are "outside the structural arrangements of a given social system." Some may also be "simultaneously members of two or more groups whose social definitions and cultural norms are distinct from and often even opposed to one another" (Turner 1974, 233).

Because of their state of marginality, ESL literacy students could also and more importantly be considered "liminars." When people are removed from families, friends, colleagues, and their normal quotidian ways of living, they experience liminality. Poised on a social and psychological tightrope, they are neither here nor there.

They are a threshold people. To greater and lesser degrees, they have separated (this rift in some ways constituting a crisis) from their mother tongue and its community. They are "betwixt and between the categories of ordinary social life." As Turner argues, liminality is "the state of being in between successive participations in social milieux dominated by social structural considerations, whether formal or unformalized" (1974, 52). Liminality is anti-structure.

Liminality may not always be the result of an accidental or spontaneous social drama. It may be planned for and deliberately entered into. Liminality enables deliberate transitions and changes in the social structures of one's life. Many cultures create liminality through rituals; neophytes and initiates often must dwell in a time and space which is consciously and carefully constructed as a threshold. Liminality may involve seclusion from everyday life in hidden places, caves, lodges in the forest, or simply in a "sheltered space and time." With a feeling of *if* and *perhaps*, of hypothesis, desire, and possibility, liminality is conducted in the subjunctive mood. It is a "privileged space where people are allowed to think about . . . the terms in which they conduct their thinking or to feel about how they feel in daily life" (1986,102). Turner provides this example from Chinese religious practices:

> [The participants were removed] from their preoccupation with small-group, convention ridden, routinized daily life and [placed] into another context of existence—the activities and feelings of the larger community. In this new orientation local inhabitants were impressed with a distinct sense of community consciousness. (Yang 1961, 89)

While everyday life may emphasize and enforce the outsiderness of the ESL literacy student, the literacy class can be constructed so as to promote liminality—the anti-structure and the betweenness. When outsiders become involved in a social process, which for Turner is ritualized and is mediated by symbols, their liminality may give rise to communitas, the kind of "community consciousness" noted above.

Communitas promotes a feeling of universality. It accomplishes this emotion through interactions that strip away the divisions and hierarchies of everyday life; communitas is marked by egalitarian relations; Turner writes:

> The bonds of communitas are anti-structural in that they are un-differentiated, equalitarian, direct, nonrational (though not irra-tional), I-Thou or Essential We relationships in Martin Buber's sense. (1974, 46)

The bond can be found in, but is not limited to, the mutual relation-ships of neophytes in initiation. It does not merge identities instead it liberates them from conformity to general norms.

Turner illustrates the movement from liminality to communitas with quotations from *The Autobiography of Malcolm X*. Malcolm X had gone on the Hadj, the traditional Muslim pilgrimage, during which he had experienced liminality because of his separation from the United States, English speakers, and the American black Muslim community. Malcolm X recounts:

> You may be shocked by these words coming from me. But on this pilgrimage, what I have seen and experienced has forced me to rearrange much of my thought-patterns previously held and to toss aside some of my previous conclusions. (1966, 340–44)

Malcolm X continues his account with testimonies of communitas "while eating, sleeping, and praying with the fellow Muslims whose hair was the blondest of blond and whose skin was the whitest of white," he began to realize that "we were truly all the same . . ." (1966, 340–44).

The move from liminality to communitas can be mediated by texts, but unless these textual interactions are socially embedded, the sense of oneness will be ephemeral. Communitas can only really be achieved in social interaction. In a liminal state, alone in a hospital bed, Carlos Bulosan read Hart Crane's poetry in his search for the universal "we" which is a kind of communitas (see Chapter 4). But these texts only nourished him temporarily, and he soon turned to reading Filipino folklore and poetry, in search, it seems, of the potential for a concrete and living communitas. As Turner argues:

> Quite often this retreat from social structure may appear to take an individualistic form, as in the case of many post-Renaissance artists, writers and philosophers. But if one looks closely at their productions, one often sees in them at least a plea for communitas. The artist is not really alone, nor does he write, paint or compose for posterity, but for living communitas. (1974, 260)

The "we" of communitas is not a "we" of ethnicity, a "we" formed with a consciousness of the Other. Turner argues that communitas "must be distinguished . . . in principle from . . . a bond between individuals who are collectively in opposition to another solidarity group." The ethnic "we" is equated with "in-group, out-group oppositions, or the we-they contrast" (Turner 1974, 202). Communitas is the "we" of universality and anti-structure, a whole which subsumes all ethnicities.

Communitas and historically sedimented social structures are related dialectically (Turner 1969, 97). The "we" of communitas has a tenuous oneness out of which social structures reassert themselves. In Turner's words, "In its genesis and central tendency, communitas is universalistic." Yet communitas moves toward the "solidarity given by bound structure" (1974, 202). Turner writes that "the historic fate of communitas seems to have been to pass from openness to closure, from "free" communitas to solidarity given by bounded structure" (1974, 202). Initiates leave the threshold in which they are all one and reenter the larger group to take their respective places in the hierarchy.

For the ESL literacy student the communitas/structure dialectic is related to, but not the same as, the universality/ethnicity dialectic that the student experiences through literacy practices in English. To review the argument for a moment, through reading and writing in English ESL students can experience universality as the negation of a "we"/Other dichotomy, as an expansion of the "we" that opposes the Other. But this experience is always dialectically related to the experience of ethnicity. Because the relationship of universality is idealistic and abstract, ethnicity, or some more particularistic and concrete sense of collectivity, is imminent. Communitas is a relationship among real human beings, not a sense of communion with a character in a book. While communitas takes place in a sheltered time and space, its chronology and location is lived, not imagined. ESL literacy practices can provide the student with the universality of communitas, but soon this unity of all will transform into some more particular "we" of ethnicity and social structures. However, the "we" of communitas is animated by and with people and their interactions with each other, rather than abstractions, as is the "we" of universality. The structure that replaces communitas is hierarchical in nature, whereas ethnicity is not necessarily encumbered with or by organized social mechanisms.

Communitas differs from the notion of discourse community that has been widely used to explain language and literacy acquisition. Communitas is dynamic, a process through which social groupings change; whereas discourse communities are conceived and discussed as static entities, not as groups which change as others join their ranks. For some theorists "joining a discourse community" connotes both the goal and the process of ESL pedagogy. Yet for many students this pedagogy of joining and assimilation fosters only liminality.

In second-language acquisition studies, while researchers seldom use the term discourse community, they do consider the issue of joining a community. In ground-breaking research on attitudes and motivation associated with second-language acquisition, psycholinguists Robert Gardner and Wallace Lambert have asked the question: "How is it that some people can learn a foreign language quickly and expertly while others, given the same opportunities to learn are utter failures?" The conclusion that they reach is that "mastering a foreign language depends on the willingness and orientation *to be like* representative members of the language community and to become associated at least vicariously with that other community" (1972, 14, emphasis added). Frank Smith, a psycholinguist and reading specialist, explains the process of learning to read and write a first language with terms and logic strikingly similar to those of Gardner and Lambert. Smith maintains that the process of becoming literate in a first language is driven by the learners desire to be like members of a community or "club" that reads and writes (1984, 2). There are two problems with these formulations. First Gardner, Lambert, and Smith suggest that language development results primarily from a state of mind in which the learner desires, or at least is willing, to emulate an Other. Second, by emphasizing the psychological, they fail to see, let alone actually describe, the social process in literacy and second-language acquisition practices.

In the field of composition there has been much talk of discourse communities. Almost all discussions employ a common vocabulary, one which suggests that these communities are actual, static entities that learners can join or "become members of":

> Most freshman English programs conceive of themselves as providing some form of introduction to university level discourse. The expectation is that students will leave English I (or whatever its designation) with the requisite reading and writing skills *to enter a new discourse community*, the world of the academy. Just what this means, however, is invariably in contention. (Roemer 1987, 911)

Most researchers describe the language that one must share to join a given discourse community. Kenneth Bruffee adds that those who share language uses in this way also form a "knowledge community," sharing not only information or facts, but values about that knowledge (1984, 644). Compositionist Patricia Bizzell sounds nearly Whorfian when she argues that those who belong to a discourse community share not only dialect features and discourse forms but also a common worldview (1986).

In all accounts, "discourse community" is an abstraction; yet some theorists reify discourse communities into clearly delineated entities that can be "joined, " thus weakening the explanatory powers of the construct itself. In these discussions, language communities are static rather than fluid. These theorists fail to recognize that discourse communities *occur* only through social interaction mediated by language. Discourse communities are constituted by actual temporal acts of language, of writing and reading. Language acts create as well as reflect social formations.

And what of the students who don't necessarily want to be like an Other, students who cherish their histories and their differences?

What of students who do not want to be "members of the club" because they perceive the club as Other? Are they to be defined as "resistant," and is this always a negative phenomenon? What can these students expect from a discourse community they do not wish to join?

Several composition theorists have tried to answer these questions. At one time Bizzell argued that joining the "academic discourse community" only seemed to suggest that students have to abandon "their own." In a rather intricate argument she contended that the academic worldview, which constitutes membership in the academic discourse community, negates other competing worldviews. But rather than argue that the academic community thus prohibits membership in other communities, she claimed that this worldview also promotes 'commitment' and encourages students to retain their alliances with home, family, neighborhood, and so forth (1986). In the end, the students might change their worldview but they would be better for it—they would be less likely to abandon their affiliations with home. Nicholas Coles and Susan Wall also want to rescue university composition from becoming a pedagogy of "initiation and assimilation" (1987, 299). They are concerned with "how [students] must become other than they are in order to accommodate our [academic] discourse." As a consequence of their concerns, they "feel the need to focus also on those motives and abilities that grow from our students' histories and that may be sustained and extended, transformed perhaps but not therefore abandoned in the process of accommodation." They conclude neither "academic discourse" nor "discourse community" can be reified:

> ". . . while we may speak broadly of the university as a 'discourse community,' particular interpretive communities come into existence only when particular students and teachers are gathered there. When this happens, neither students nor teachers leave their histories behind; they bring them to class, to every academic discussion, and to every reading and writing assignment. (Coles and Wall 1987, 313)

To reiterate, the "joining" metaphor is capable of reproducing rather than negating liminality for ESL students. A pedagogy which even tacitly assumes that students must join "us" and be like "us" to be valorized as readers and writers alienates and silences because it does not allow students to create communitas and multiple mutable communities.

I want to advocate a pedagogy in which communitas is both a goal and a method. As discussed above, most adult second-language learners encounter liminality. Without communitas, liminality creates alienation and despair. Gardner and Lambert have discussed this phenomenon with respect to second-language acquisition. They have used Durkheim's term anomie to describe the second-language learner's sense of outsiderness (1972, 16–7). In a pedagogy of communitas, ESL literacy practices acquire their value because they enable a dialectic, a back and forthness, between the worlds of native speakers and the worlds of ethnic communities; for Carlos Bulosan, adult education students, Chinua Achebe, and university students, ESL literacy practices contributed to the "we" of ethnicity as well as to its transformation.

By arguing that the ESL literacy class can engage participants in a communitas of universality, I do not mean to imply that the "we" of ethnicity is to be shunned; its abnegation is not the goal of the ESL literacy class. The social goal of the ESL literacy class is the negation of anomie. It is important to remember that because ethnicity and universality are dialectically related, they continually work to transform each other. The "we" of universality is anti-structural while the "we" of ethnicity asserts recognized structures.

Within communitas, people find motivation for action and change. Communitas promotes change by carrying participants across social boundaries, providing them with the experience of insiderhood, enabling them to create new cultural ideals. Both in and out of the classroom, ESL students may return to the "we" of ethnicity. The experience of communitas, however, will "help to mitigate and assuage some of the abrasiveness of social conflicts" (Turner 1974, 56); communitas removes the "sting of the structural domain" (Turner 1974, 260). Turner writes further that after the experience of communitas, "man ... can never again be quite so parochial, so particularistic in his social loyalties" (1974, 260). When communitas gives away to structure, new relations may have formed, "oppositions may be found to have become alliances and vice versa. Asymmetric relations may have become egalitarian ones and so on" (Turner 1974, 42). Communitas allows for new cultural ideals and a multiplicity of selves to be formed as the metaphors that direct one's activities change (Turner 1986, 59).

Pedagogy of Mediation

Before looking specifically at ideas for ESL literacy pedagogy, I want to clarify what mediation has to do with what teachers and students do in classes. To do this, I want to contrast two literacy pedagogies based, at least in part, on the construct of mediation, two very different notions of mediation—the pedagogy of Ann Berthoff and that of Paulo Freire. Contrasting these two should bring to mind again the differences between the assumptions and activities of individualist and social literacy pedagogies.

Much as Sapir and Whorf argued that language mediates thought, some literacy specialists contend that literacy not only shapes but improves thought. Compositionists Cy Knoblauch and Lil Brannon, for example, argue that "the value of writing in any course should lie in its power to enable the discovery of knowledge" (1983, 466). The writing-across-the-disciplines movement in composition promotes the use of writing in all disciplines with the premise that writing mediates learning.

Ann Berthoff has perhaps the most carefully articulated version of this position. She begins with the premise that "language [is] an instrument of knowing" (1982, 45). She conceives of cognition and perception as conjoined interpretive acts that are mediated by language. While language and thought may be related dialectically, language is privileged. Language has "form-finding and form-creating" powers. Berthoff argues that "form finds form" (1982, 2). Literacy is language. She talks about *language* in one sentence and in the next phrase, the term *language* has been replaced by *writing* or *composing*. Berthoff slips literacy into her argument without arguing. For her, language and literacy are nearly the same. She writes as though all of the generalized powers she attributes to all of language use can be laid on top of reading and writing. She completely eliminates the need for thinking about such things as the contexts, people, histories, purposes of literacy. Berthoff claims that "[Writing] is a matter . . . of learning how to use the forms of language to discover the forms of thought and vice versa" (1982, 46). Social interaction is completely missing from these pictures of literacy and its mediating qualities. Words and brains, forms finding forms, float about in space.

In the pedagogy which emerges from these ideas, writer and reader are treated as monads who examine repeatedly their own thought processes—"thinking about thinking" (Berthoff 1982, 41), "observing your observations" (Berthoff 1982, 12). Language mediates thought. Thought mediates literacy. Fundamentally, thought, literacy, and language are all properties of the individual. Man is the forming animal, "the animal symbolicum," as Ernst Cassirer puts it, and composing, as the act of an individual, naturally entails reflection which is by definition beneficial (Berthoff 1982, 2).

This picture of mediation is of limited use in constructing a pedagogy of ESL literacy. As argued at length throughout this book, ESL literacy practices cannot be adequately understood as acts of the brain, as behaviors of isolated individuals. This is not to claim that language does not mediate thought for ESL writers and readers. It is to argue that language mediates acts of second-language literacy through "intrapsychological processes which are social in their genesis" (Vygotsky 1981, 163).

The literacy pedagogy of Brazilian educator Paulo Freire is also grounded in the mediating qualities of language. Freire, however, adds a social dimension to the equation of thought and language, recognizing that language mediates social interaction and social interaction mediates "thought." While Berthoff (1982, 45) argues that "language is an *instrument* of knowing," Freire proposes that "the literacy process, as cultural action for freedom, is an *act* of knowing in which the learner assumes the role of knowing subject in dialogue with the educator" (1970, 369, emphasis added).

In Freire's educational scheme, dialogue among the students and the coordinator is mediated by "codifications," texts in the form of pictures and "generative" words which represent scenes and issues that are significant in the students' lives. In Freire's terms:

> Codification, on the one hand, mediates between the concrete and the theoretical contexts (of reality). On the other hand, as knowable object, it mediates between the knowing subjects, educators and learners, who seek in dialogue to unveil the action-object wholes. (1970, 371)

Crucially, Freire emphasizes the actions and the relationships of the participants in the literacy process rather than the inert properties of language or innate capacities of "man."

Codifications mediate in two ways: they mediate representation and they mediate dialogue or interaction among students and teacher(s). With the codifications, students are able to represent their lives. They "read" the representation, the image in the codification, and they "write" about it. Dialogue mediates the reading and writing which focuses on generative words. Put in other terms, the codifications are the basis for dialogue, and social interaction is the basis of dialogue. In considering the mediating qualities of language and literacy for ESL writers and readers, it is important to note that social interaction can either facilitate or inhibit literacy practices. Literacy practices acquire their liberatory or their oppressive characteristics through the social interactions that they mediate.

While some theorists imply that composing, or reading, is an inherently creative, enriching, and transforming act, Freire, in contrast, argues that the salutary effects of literacy depend on dialogue among students and teachers. "True dialogue," Freire argues, "unites subjects together in the cognition of a knowable object which mediates between them" (1970, 369). Freire also recognizes that without dialogue the process can be used to dominate:

Insofar as the primer is the mediating object between the teacher and the students, and the students are to be "filled" with words the teachers have chosen, one can easily detect a first important dimension of the image of man which here begins to emerge. It is the profile of man whose consciousness is "spatialized" and must be filled or fed in order to know. (1970, 371)

Students should not be taught through prepared primers or textbooks, which put teachers in the role of "bankers" who own, control, and disperse language, the knowledge to be learned. In "banking education" students are not subjects in their own educational process but objects dominated by the process itself (Freire 1982, 57–74). In Freire's scheme the dialogue that is the basis of social interaction is between subjects. In Freire's work, as in any pedagogy which considers mediation fully, language mediates thought, but both thought and language are social through and through.

Effective Classroom Practices

The ESL class can use a dialectic of communitas (or anti-structure) and social structure to make ESL students conscious of how the pushes and pulls of ethnicity and universality affect their literacy practices, their language, and their educational development. In an effective ESL literacy class, not only will students experience the "we's" of ethnicity *and* universality, but they will also become aware of how literacy and language mediate these emotions and relations.

By now it may be obvious that I view reading and writing (literacy) to be interdependent with oral language uses. Yet many ESL materials artificially focus on one "skill"—i.e., reading, suggesting that the essence of reading can be separated from speaking and writing. The materials imply that speaking about, before, while, and after reading are inconsequential addenda to "reading," not a vital part of the activity itself. Most teachers, of course, do have their students speak and read and write together, but they may be wary of having students talk too much in their reading classes. I prefer the term literacy because it denotes the interdependence of orality and reading and writing. The classes described below "work" because the teachers perceive and encourage just this interdependency. They also recognize that all language use is social; reading and writing are not primarily cognitive, individualist activities.

Below I list some of the attributes of ESL literacy classes that invoke communitas. Woven through this inventory of principles are stories of ESL literacy classes which illustrate not only how successes are achieved, but also how they are defined. This list of characteristics for effective classes is by no means complete, nor are the examples of effective practices. What follows are suggestive guidelines rather than a comprehensive catalog.

1. *The social relationships and social interactions among students and between student(s) and teacher are fundamental to the success of the class. The social relations mediate literacy, and this literacy process engenders a dialectic of communitas and structure. The class should experience not only a spontaneous but normative communitas which is not random or unexpected, but routine, developed as part of the ongoing relations of the course.*

Teachers should focus on social interactions in the class as much if not more than "the material" to be covered. Along these lines, class materials should not be treated as inflexible static texts, but as suggestions for teacher and student interactions. In ESL literacy, especially in those classes aimed at "beginning" readers and writers, much of the published materials is labeled "learner-centered"; the assumption is that the materials address the needs of the students. Yet, all too often these materials have been developed by a teacher rather than by teachers and students together. These prepared materials are meant to be controlled by a teacher who assigns and collects them. In such a class, interaction is not considered a serious component of the pedagogy, and the students act not as a group but as an aggregate of individuals. Among some students, particularly those who interact in English only in class, the "banking" education described above engenders resistance, passivity (non-engagement). This class contributes little to the students' literacy and language development. American interpreters of Freire's work, Nan Elsasser and Vera John-Steiner argue that "true communication demands equality between speakers and this often requires an alteration in current social relationships" (1987, 47).

Collaborative learning techniques are important ways of changing the social relationships which students bring into the class from the world. In the classes described below, the students work in groups to produce texts which they share with each other. Linda Blanton's *Idea Exchange* provides an example:

> Situations can be set up in the classroom where students collaborate with each other as partners to share their histories aloud. As they listen to each other, they become conscious of differences and similarities between their own histories and those of their partners. (Blanton 1990, 2)

After the small group activity, the students share their texts with the whole class. "When the writing is ready, it forms a pool of texts for the class to read. Twenty texts or so are passed around the room, and students are encouraged to exchange ideas or comments with the writers themselves" (Blanton 1990, 2). These activities require that students participate with each other in ways that they may not outside the class.

In collaborative activities students with very different abilities and experiences in English and literacy can work together in groups. Some may work in their native languages. The group can translate. Beginning students may dictate their thoughts, and other students or the teacher can act as a scribe. Even when the students are working independently of each other, they retain a sense of the group.

The rituals of the class, of group work, help to create normative, ongoing communitas. When the teacher is a collaborator rather than the director of the class, much of the other classroom ritual can be turned over to the students: attendance, announcements, distribution of work, and so forth. In addition, group rituals that ask students and teacher to think about (describe, analyze, evaluate) the group experience and their own role in the group help to level differences among participants and build group cohesion simultaneously. Nina Wallerstein, an American interpreter of Freire, asks students and teachers together to evaluate their own learning, to reflect as a group: "Did the code tap a generative familiar theme? Did the room come to life with students' emotions, laughter and stories? Did it foster student understanding of the causes of the problem and was action taken?" She argues that assessment can be a powerful tool when "students evaluate their own learning and reflect as a group on the actions they have taken" (1987, 44).

I would add that this self-evaluation can be an important activity for normative communitas. Wallerstein's version of a "problem-posing" "participatory curriculum" engenders communitas. The literacy practices of the classroom create a "we." At first, the referent for the feeling of community may be limited to the members of the class, yet as Turner argues "communitas pushes to universality" (1969, 202). This local "we" is the basis for a more broadly defined community.

Social interaction needs to be taken into account not just in the materials, the curriculum, and the classroom activities, but in the very program design itself. Rather than design classes for heterogeneous collections of individuals, administrators and teachers can take advantage of the social networks which already exist in a community. Rather than offer a class at a school site, ESL literacy groups could be formed among friends and neighbors at community centers, churches, small local businesses. Family literacy projects, for example, reflect "a growing concern for ways in which families affect and create the conditions for literacy development and use. In projects such as Learning English through Intergenerational Friendship (LEIF), the aim is to use "language and literacy to 'heal' social divisions among generations and break down the isolation of refugee elders" (Weinstein-Shr 1989, 9).

One Story

Kyle Fiore and Nan Elsasser (1987) tell the story of a course in basic writing taught in the Bahamas. Their narrative illustrates how teachers and students can productively engage in a dialectic of universality and ethnicity that results in communitas.

Soon after the Bahamian basic writing course began, the teacher asked the students to write on "What You Need to Know to Live in the Bahamas," a topic important to her as a neophyte in the culture. Even though this assignment appears to be grounded in students' everyday worlds, they found it difficult to "step outside immediate contextual realities and incorporate broader points of view." The students couldn't easily imagine what the teacher would want or need to know. One woman who wrote "a recipe for conch salad assumed that conch [was] a familiar food" (Fiore and Elsasser 1987, 91).

As students worked on this difficult topic, together they would "develop the basic procedure . . . to investigate a generative theme":

> First, we discuss the topic at hand. . . . Then one student volunteers a thesis statement related to the topic. Other women help narrow and sharpen this statement and develop an essay outline. Students use these guidelines for their drafts. I reproduce the drafts, and we read and comment on them. After prolonged discussion, each woman rewrites her draft to meet the questions we've raised. (Fiore and Elsasser 1987, 92)

Through this discussion "students take on more and more responsibility for the class" (1987, 92). The topic helps to level differences of author-ity between students and teacher. This equality encourages students to appropriate language. Through collaborative drafting, the students share knowledge, and as they become conscious that *they* indeed know what one "needs to know to live in the Bahamas," they acknowledge, at least tacitly, their similarities. The topic and the collaborative writing process lay the grounds for communitas, a "we" within the class.

Next, the teacher turned to her students for help in coming up with "generative themes," "issues from their daily lives that they would like to talk, read and write about for the semester" (Fiore and Elsasser 1987, 92). The students brought in ideas, the teacher listed them on the board, the class talked about the choices and voted, selecting the topic of "marriage." The students broke into groups to develop lists of subtopics on which they could focus.

The teacher put together a packet of readings related to the subtopics: *Our Bodies Ourselves* by the Boston Women's Health Collective, articles from *New Woman* and *Ebony,* a novel about marriage in India, *Nectar in a Sieve,* by Kamala Markandaya. As the students sorted through the readings they "found much of value in *Our Bodies Ourselves*" . . . and they "dismiss[ed] poet Judith Viorst as a spoiled middle-class housewife" (Fiore and Elsasser 1987, 93). Through reading these Other texts, not their own or those of their classmates, the students came to "perceive stronger links between their own lives and the larger social context." Through reading, they constructed an Other: Viorst, middle class, spoiled, etc., and through their discussions of Viorst and her concerns, reading mediated their construction of a "we." These readings were "a basis for dialogues about individual problems, *common experiences, and the larger social world*" (Fiore and Elsasser 1987, 93, emphasis added). The readings would be used as "a bridge" between "students' lives and society." Readings, in other words, were used, not only to construct the local "we" of "common experiences," but also to move students toward the communitas which pushes toward universality, the communitas of the "larger social world."

Throughout the semester, the women "seiz[ed] more control in class and start[ed] to generate their own theories on the writing mechanics" (Fiore and Elsasser 1987, 97). They appropriated language. They did not wait passively for the teacher to pass out rules to be patiently practiced and mimicked. The students were not solipsistic about language. They even retained the concept of error and correctness, but they "hypothesize[d] the rules themselves" (Fiore and Elsasser 1987, 97). This difference is significant. When the teacher controls the knowledge, the language, boundaries between the students and the Other solidify. The Other is reified in the process. Students perceive a barrier to literacy practices and language development. To become engaged in ESL literacy, students need to experience the permeability of Other-ness by appropriating the Other's language in communitas.

As the course went on, the students began "to use writing as a means of intervening in their own social environment" (Fiore and Elsasser 1987, 93). They decided to write together "an open letter to Bahamian men" for the island newspapers. Their composing procedures remained the same: students wrote individual drafts; they gathered to discuss these letters and outline a collective letter; each student chose to draft a subtopic from the outline; they edited; they went "line by line . . . spending over an hour on each page" (Fiore and Elsasser 1987, 100).

The amazing end to this amazing story is that when the semester ended, the women continued to meet. "They read about women in *other* countries, *broaden*[ed] their understandings, and wrote a resource book for *Bahamian* women" (Fiore and Elsasser 1987, 100). The Other, the universal, and the local, the ethnic "we," are present in these continuing meetings, in these continuing literacy practices.

2. Introduce multiple voices into the class, including the voice of the Other.

In many "learner-centered" ESL curricula, students read only their "own" texts and those of their classmates. Freire writes that there is no place for primers, not even "good ones" in his educational scheme. Some interpreters of Freire believe that the voices of the teacher and the students in dialogue will be enough to bring about the "critical consciousness" which abnegates the "culture of silence" (Freire 1970, 367). But as Freire recognizes, literacy does not develop out of an individual inner organic seed. Literacy grows out of inter-action, and part of that interaction should be with texts which are alien to the ongoing dialogue, texts which interject the conflicting voice.

I am not arguing that students will themselves evolve into writing like the Other, abnegating their previous viewpoints, languages, and texts. This is not an assimilationist argument. Perhaps this point can be clarified by contrasting the dialectical argument with the as-similationism of Sylvia Ashton Warner. She envisions "organic liter-acy" as a first step or stage in the literacy process. For "organic literacy" the reading has to be in "sympathy" with the students; it has to have "incident which they understand and temperament which they sense. Only in a familiar atmosphere can reading be evolution-ary" (Ashton Warner 1963, 63). Yet Ashton Warner sees organic liter-acy as a step which will lead students to appreciate standard reading materials, in particular the "Janet and John" series. Ashton Warner herself created transitional books to "lead up to" this series by draw-ing from the thousands of organic texts which her students wrote in "the language of the pa." She believes that when students can learn to read and write from the "Janet and John" books, she will have contributed to their "social stability." The dialectic perspective does not envision the student evolving into the Other, but instead always pushing against the Other and, with this push and pull, creating multiple writing and reading languages and selves.

As the students in Fiore and Elsasser's story searched for an English to which they could commit themselves, they benefited from exposure to Other voices, discussions in which Other texts could be felt and examined for their habits of language, politics, and senti-ment. In reading and writing with Other texts, texts other than their own and those of their classmates, students find language, new ver-sions of English, to appropriate. When students can be nourished by the foreign qualities of Other-ness, Other-ness breaks down.

A Second Story

This is a story about an ESL class that was part of an adult literacy project in Los Angeles. The students were young, eighteen to twenty-three years old. They were from Vietnam, Central America, Cam-bodia, and Mexico. They had all lived in the United States for several years. None had high school diplomas, and some had had as little as three years of formal schooling. All had attended at least a few months of ESL classes, but none spoke much English. My "class" with these students was part of a literacy project which was, in turn, part of a state work-training program. This story shows how even beginning students can use literacy to mediate the social interaction that they require for language acquisition and for literacy practices to have meaning themselves.

Each morning when the students assembled in the classroom at seven, I would already have written messages on the blackboard. Some were as simple as "Good Morning. How are you today?" Others were more complex: Dear Students, Every day I hear everybody talk-ing about mclouds. What is a mcloud? Is it alive? Is it dangerous? Let me know, OK?" The students would hover about the board, struggling to read the words aloud. Eventually, they would request my participation by calling out simply "teacher." Then Jorge or Va together would manage to read "How are you"; they would follow the reading with a smile and answer "OK, work easy day" or "No good, dirty boots, supervisor dock me."

The messages were not structured so as to teach specific lexical or syntactic structures. They were not the basis of carefully "con-trolled" language lessons. I asked questions that I really wanted the answers to. However, even when the students did not know many or any of the words, they did not ignore the blackboard missives; they did not have to be asked to read the notes. Instead they all gathered to collaboratively read, and often to write answers back. This collab-orative approach to reading at the board and all writing activities as well seemed to be a catalyst to the students' willingness to engage with me and with each other in English.

The students wrote, spoke, and read because the social roles and expectations of the literacy group participants differed significantly from those of both the workplace and the traditional ESL class. In both previous ESL classes and their current work, the students were expected to accept and follow direction without question; they had little input as to how their time would be spent. Dialectically, reading and writing facilitated the social interactions of the literacy group, and these interactions promoted reading and writing.

In my class, the students were never given assignments. They did not practice the "sub-skills" of reading and writing. They did not do exercises. The table next to the board was covered with writing materials (pens and paper, folders and notebooks, butcher paper and magic markers), and print (newspapers, magazines and books—some in English, some in Chinese, Vietnamese, and Spanish). I read to them and they read to me. Most of the books were real—stories, poems, comics, or essays—and some were fake, textbook-like readers. I had cut up ESL readers, eliminating all of the vocabulary lists and comprehension questions, yet preserving the stories. Over several months one of the students used an altered copy of *No Hot Water Tonight* (Bodman 1975), an ESL reader about life in the inner city, as a model to write about his car. He called his masterpiece "No Car Start Tonight," and when he had finished it, he read the two pages to the group.

I would suggest activities to the students, but sometimes they acted as though they were sleepy, and, if they did, no one interfered with them. Many of them had to get up before five to get to work on time. More often than not, however, the sleep scenario would go like this: Teresa would stroll in, glare, and put her head down on the desk. Some of the other students would be collaborating on a story about Chinese New Year. One would transcribe on the board and he and others would argue about the names in English for Chinese traditional foods. It would be noisy, and eventually Teresa would raise her head and spit out: "I no wetback." I would ask Teresa to elaborate on her outburst, but probably she wouldn't. She would probably have put her head back on the desk, or she may have asked the Vietnamese students about their story. She probably wouldn't have talked to the group about the events that had precipitated her outburst, at least not that day. Maybe a week or two later, she would raise that topic of "wetbacks" again, and through a combination of writing and talking with me and a couple of other classmates, she would work out a story about a grocery store clerk who hadn't understood her English and had called her a wetback.

What is of particular interest here is my role as a teacher collaborating in Teresa's making of meaning. In basic agreement with Paulo Freire, Kenneth Bruffee has suggested that the social relations among the teacher and the students must be realigned in collaborative learning. The teacher becomes a "metteur en scene whose responsibility and privilege is to arrange optimum conditions for other people to learn" (1984, 470). With these students, arranging these "optimum conditions" involved me in what M.A.K. Halliday has called "tracking," a social interaction in which an adult or teacher shares in the language creating with the child or student (Harste 1984, 61). Tracking includes helping students find new ways to say things as they discover new reasons to express themselves or understand others. To the basic concept of tracking, Vygotsky adds the perspective that cooperation between a children and adults or teachers and students can lead students to what they could not yet do by themselves.

About four months after the start of the literacy group, I suggested that the students start a newspaper for all the other classes to read. At first the students responded negatively. They wanted nothing to do with any newspaper. They were the only group of non-native speakers in the literacy project. They claimed they couldn't write; they didn't know enough English, and so forth. But I persisted. I interviewed Va, a Chinese/Vietnamese man, about events and people in which I knew he was interested. I enlisted another student to help with the interview and the writing. In elaborate, slow, and deliberate steps, the students and I translated to and from their native languages to get the story on paper. Then, I typed and duplicated the interview, listing both my name and the students' names as the writers. The next day I asked Va to read the story aloud to the group. He did, with the help of two friends. Seeing that he was obviously pleased to read his story, I asked if I could make his interview the first issue of the newspaper. And thus, the group began what they were to entitle "The Friendship News."

As a group they would write out interview questions. Most were as simple as "What is your favorite food?" Then they would go to other literacy classes, asking permission to come in and interview the class members. They might announce themselves as abruptly as "interview" or "the newspaper." They might even give the native speaking students their questions and a piece of paper on which to write their answers and names.

When they returned to the haven of their own class, they would pore over their answers, reading again and again, asking questions like—what is steak? The explanation of steak would lead to a discussion of why Americans eat so much beef and so little rice or so few tortillas.

Not only did social interaction mediate these literacy practices, but through the newspaper the students had learned to use literacy to mediate social interaction. The newspaper had provided a context for these young people to create relationships which previously they had been uninterested in or shut out of. The newspaper promoted their language development, not because of the specific language practice it required of the students, but because of the social interactions it involved them in, interactions that required language. The students had learned to use literacy practices to be involved in their environment—the literacy group, the literacy project at large, their work training program.

The students did not seem to want to emulate an abstract community of English readers and writers, they had little image of a "literacy club" (Smith 1984), one that they certainly had had even less contact with. When these ESL students were involved in the social and symbolic activities of writing and reading, they found the grounds for interpreting their experiences as a "we" of universality, the "we" of communitas.

Communitas is of several types. Within the classroom, when social interactions mediated by literacy practices produce radical social change, students may experience spontaneous communitas, a oneness with all. The students created relationships with each other, with me. They invited me to their homes; they visited mine. Va and I talked for hours and hours about dreams and goals, family, food, cars, and adventures. Carmen gave Duc a journal to write in for his birthday, and he accepted it graciously. They began to ask questions about racism in the United States, to talk to and discuss their ideas with their Black colleagues in the program. This original communitas, or experience of fellowship, may be organized into a perduring system of normative communitas, through the rituals of the class and small group work. Normative communitas remains anti-structural. The rituals work against the hierarchical grain; they do not reinstitute social divisions. The students organized group meetings, panel discussions, about problems in their new community formation.

The students from the narrative above provide an example. The nonnative speakers clearly experienced themselves as outsiders in the English speaking world and even in their work training program. By collaborating with each other and their teacher in writing and reading activities, the process of communitas could begin. It was, I believe, crucial that reading and writing were collaborative activities, meaning the students both wrote together and discussed the texts that they and others had written. It was also crucial that I not act as a "banker" (Freire 1982), there to fill them up with the knowledge that I, and I alone in the group, possessed. Instead I was a collaborator. This did not mean that I had to negate my knowledge, or any of my differences from the students, any more than it required that the students become like me. It did mean that I was not an arbiter of what was to be said and how it was to be said; instead, I contributed my knowledge when asked by the rest of the group.

These collaborative activities stripped away the hierarchies of everyday life, leaving room for the anti-structure of communitas. The Hispanic and Asian students entered the class suspicious of and hostile to each other. These attitudes were not evident when they worked together on the newspaper, which they decided to call the "Friendship News." Their collaboration in creating and distributing texts leveled differences among them.

Their writing engendered interaction with the native speakers in the literacy project. If the native speakers noticed that the nonnatives spoke or wrote in nonstandard English, they never mentioned it. Instead they would approach Jorge or Va to ask about the war in Nicaragua and the location of Vietnam. Soon the ESL writers would go from literacy group to literacy group asking the native speakers if they had anything to contribute to the newspaper. Because they had distributed their newspaper to the students at large, the nonnative speakers had become visible as a group, as an asserted "we." This "we," however, dissolved when the ESL students chose to include the native speakers writing in their newspaper. When the nonnative speakers interacted with others, their community grew.

3. Literacy practices are part of the world. The world is the class.

Students need experiences with literacy practices, not language exercises. Work with paragraphs, sentences, grammar, and comprehension exercises in itself does not lead students to become engaged either in literacy or in the interactions mediated by literacy. Exercises do not accomplish literacy. Literacy accomplishes literacy.

To develop activities for their students, teachers should begin not with the "skill" they want to inculcate, but with the things that people do with and through literacy in the world. They should model their curricula not on the practices of school, but on those of everyday life.

The classes described above did not do exercises, or modules, or workbooks. They didn't read poetry only to do grammar exercises developed out of the poems. The literacy classes gained their inspiration from the world, not from schools. The classrooms were literacy environments, and the world was the class. The literacy of the class, the attendance and other record keeping, was done by the students. The tables were covered with newspapers and magazines. The students had organized a small paperback library in a box. With real reading materials, students interacted the way writers and readers interact in the world. They talked about what they read; they sat in circles, around tables, and off by themselves (but never in rows). They became excited or frustrated and even sometimes bored. But they did not just passively sit. The learners did not do assigned work in groups; they did not read assigned Robert Louis Stevenson poems and do comprehension questions. They made signs with slogans of encouragement in bold letters (*Si se puede*), which they posted on bulletin boards. They wrote up and sent out reminders about class birthday celebrations. They chose a class poet. They wrote poems as gifts. They started a tamale business and organized potlucks. They learned about pesticides in the fields. They raised money for books. They learned that when people do these things together, they often do these things with and through literacy.

Story Three

A while ago I worked with migrant agricultural workers. Some had been here a long time, some not so long. Some were legally here; some were applying for amnesty. Many had had several years of education in Mexico, yet they spoke English falteringly. Others spoke with confidence yet balked at reading and writing in English. All were anxious about their English or their literacy, but generally, even the newcomers had a tentative sense of security in their lives here. The patterns of migration, the habits and histories of moving with the crops were old. When individuals crossed the river to pick in the strawberry fields, they found a way of life that had been maintained for decades by their compatriots.

In an old church basement near the fields, my friend Christina taught an ESL class after the students' day of work. The class began by talking, in Spanish and in English, about why they were taking ESL and what they wanted from the class. At first, their statements were formulaic: to learn English, to get a better job. They talked and talked. They enjoyed telling their stories. Christina took notes on poster board paper and made outlines of the times, places, and people in their lives: Jorge—Crystal City, Texas, to Kenosha, Wisconsin. Three sons. She pasted the outlines on the wall. The atmosphere was easy. The students brought food and slumped back in their chairs.

Eventually Christina suggested that the students think of the class as storytelling time. It was a concept broad enough to invite individuals to talk about the ins and outs of their various days, and encourage them to recover and revision their histories and futures. Her suggestion was met with strange looks, remarks of "Sure, teacher," and shrugs.

She divided the students into groups and asked them to think of the stories, or types of stories they wanted to tell—about everyday life in the fields, about encounters in Anglo worlds, about life histories of grandparents, aunts, and uncles, about migrations, baptisms, and religious conversions. They did. They wrote long lists on the poster paper, which again she pasted to the wall.

Some students were worried about learning English for very specific purposes: The foundry on 8th street would hire again in June, paying twelve dollars an hour for those who could pass the English test. Christina said that she would call and try to find out what the test consisted of. She reassured these students that the class would address their needs.

The next class Christina began by asking if anyone had heard a story called *Bless Me Ultima* by Rudolfo Anaya. Briefly she recounted the outlines of the tale: a young boy Tony was caught between two worlds. His father's family wandered with the cows of the range; his mother's family tended the land in one place. Tony was pulled in two directions—everyday he lived with the talismans of the *curanderas* and the holy cards and rosaries of Catholicism. Tony's father told the confused boy to "reform the old materials to make something." Tony took this advice to heart, repeating to himself the following litany for survival: "Make something new . . . take the llano, the river valley, the moon and the sea, God the Golden carp— and make something new" (Anaya 1972, 236). The class talked about Tony and how their lives too were pulled in many directions.

To everyone's surprise, the students took Tony's story to heart. The aphorism for the class was "make something new." One group made several posters with this saying in huge bright letters. As they told their stories, they were conscious of new materials, new contexts, new audiences which would change the shape of the story- telling. For example, several members of a family wrote their family history, interviewing aunts, uncles, a grandmother, and some children. They wrote it in Spanish because this was the language spoken in the interviews. It was the language "natural" to this con- text. Then, with help and encouragement from other classmates, they decided to rewrite it, to make it new, in English so that their children could take it to school. They wanted the history to be accu- rate and as "warm" in English as it was in Spanish, so they labored over the English text. They did not worry about its correctness in the terms of some abstract standard. They were concerned about how it sounded and how it felt, about its connotations and nuances. When they were finished, some of the text remained in Spanish because the students had decided that some quotations were not translatable.

They told stories and made new stories, new plans, new written texts. Other students rewrote Mexican folktales or folk proverbs in English. They retold histories of Mexico, especially chapters on the Revolution and information on migrant workers, which they had found on their trip to the public library. They wrote tall tales about their accomplishments on the job, about dreams of mansions with swimming pools. Christina read aloud to them *Through Harsh Winters*, the story of a Japanese migrant worker (Kikumura 1981). They compared their experiences with hers.

Although she could not obtain any information about the English test at the foundry, the students were not particularly worried. They tackled the problem themselves discussing what they might ask in such a test. They asked if such a test were legal. They practiced telling their stories. They role played boss, tester, and test taker. Then, they began to think about the questions they might like to ask such as: How hot does it get in the foundry? Can I change shifts?

In groups and individually, they wrote and read and talked. Whether in English or Spanish or some combination, the texts and the interactions which produced them helped the students to form a community, a "we."

4. Students choose and make their own learning materials.

The classes described above share a *project approach* to literacy education. In this type of class, the students decide on a project(s) that they want to do together. The project may focus on producing a text such as a letter to the newspaper, a resource guide (see Fiore/Elsasser discussion above), a class/school newspaper, oral histories. Or, students may choose to organize a community day care center or a basketball league, clean up the neighborhood park, protest the change of school boundaries, or some other social action. In this second group of projects, texts themselves are usually not the end goal. Texts mediate the actions of the project. This approach is similar to the idea of a "generative theme" of Freirean pedagogy, but here action is not the last step in a sequence of activities, it is the starting place, the goal, the center piece of the class. Once chosen, the project generates all of the work of the class. Students organize time lines for publication, write letters, make phone calls, do interviews, and make signs and logos. The students read, write, and talk. This is the work of the class.

While they are involved in accomplishing their project, they may want, need, and choose to read the writing of others. Just as *Our Bodies Ourselves* and Judith Viorst were useful, in very different ways, to the women in the Bahamian class, so reading can help students to define what they are doing, to see how they can accomplish their goals. This is very different from classes in which the teacher picks the readings for their language value, and the readings have little or no connection to each other or to the students' interests.

In the examples described above students published their writing—they made it public. They wrote letters to the editor and made newspapers, resource books, and bulletin boards. They produced public readings, oral histories, community log books, scrapbooks, chapbooks, stories for children, coloring books, recipe books. "When students publish their writings, they have the opportunity to see their own thoughts and concerns, and those of others like them, represented in print. They have a voice both within and beyond the classroom" (Peyton 1989). These voices and these rituals of publication helped to define the "we" of the class, engendering communitas "both within and beyond."

In the same vein it is good for students to read the writing of other students. Many adult literacy programs are now publishing their own students' writing. "Student-produced materials can form a *body of contemporary knowledge* closely tied to the lives of the people reading them and providing inspiration to students to write their own stories" (Peyton 1989). The "knowledge" which published student texts make manifest contributes to community formation.

5. Language acquisition is language appropriation.

Bakhtin writes: "The period of national languages, coexisting but closed and deaf to each other, [has come] to an end" (1986, 12). Languages are interanimated (1986, 51). These literacy classes problematized the goal of acquiring a set standard English because they also questioned the very idea of a unified and static standard language. The students were asked to notice and think about the multiplicity of Englishes. These students learned to "build a superstructure over these languages made up of [their] own intentions and accents" (Bakhtin 1981, 409). Theirs was not an "autotelic parodying" (Bakhtin 1981, 509). They learned to animate the word with their own context; they did not write as though they were taking dictation, hoping to get it right. They did not wait for others to dole out the rules. Yet they were encouraged to investigate issues of "correctness" and rules. Questions of "Is this right?" were transformed into discussions about the very notion of "right" in a language. The idea of a language, with definite and stable borders, was seriously questioned.

Cultural critic Colin MacCabe interprets James Joyce in such a way as to suggest that he could provide a model for ESL students— not of texts to imitate, but of his aims to emulate. MacCabe argues that Joyce's project was a "prolonged interrogation of an alien language . . . a subversion of those cultural and linguistic forms which offer identity only in the accents of the ruler. [Joyce] uses other cultures and languages to break open and reveal the contradiction in his own" (1988, 12). ESL students can use their own languages and cultures to reveal the tensions in English and American culture. Joyce intended to use what MacCabe calls "Broken English." Students can be taught to craft their texts not only to duplicate standard English but to break it.

The migrant workers wrote bilingual texts. In the collaborative texts, language was demonstrably not the property of an individual. These texts mingled the languages of all their composers. As Ian Pringle writes, ". . . we have no choice but to acknowledge that what we used to call English belongs as well to those whose mother tongue is some other language. Our challenge is to accept the logical consequences of that recognition. We must recognize that English as language is not only the varieties spoken by us in our own countries, but all varieties . . ." (1985, 130).

Even when *teachers* believe in such a project, it is difficult to effect this change of attitude in students. They are accustomed to the idea that in language there is a right and a wrong, clear-cut distinctions that the teacher knows and affirms. For the very reason that it is so hard to unseat this authority of the teacher over language and to disturb the notion of language as a thing which belongs to someone, it is vitally important to try. It does not happen immediately. Reading differently disturbs deep-seated ideologies and habits of meaning. (See Chapter 6 for a vocabulary for reading the voices of ESL literacy.)

University Composition

What does all of the above mean for the English course, the university composition course? The classes discussed above were situated in adult education settings rather than in universities. What value(s) would a pedagogy of communitas assign to academic discourse? If collaborative learning is crucial to communitas, how are students and instructors in the university to collaborate? Furthermore, what are the textual results of communitas—that is, how can we characterize the writing and reading that is produced?

The freshman English class is not so very different from the adult education class. In fact, university composition would do well to initiate the types of projects and collaborative learning that I have suggested for adult education classes. (Ironically, all too often adult education classes mimic the worst of university composition classes—contextless, nearly nonsensical exercises and writing assignments.)

Even in freshman English, communitas can occur through projects and collaborative learning. Students can compile student guides to the campus and the area, international student newsletters, study guides for textbooks, books of student essays, and responses to anthologized essays. They can interview other nonnative speakers living in the area, small business owners, restaurant owners, and publish these oral histories. They can publish reviews of university courses. Students can tutor English speakers in their native languages (Spanish, for example), or in math and computer science.

Students can be involved in choosing readings: pieces translated from their home languages; articles and novels, such as Jamaica Kincaid's *Lucy* about the experience of recognizing yet not understanding an "Other" perspective (1991). Contemporary novels such as *No Telephone to Heaven* (Cliff 1989) can be used to illustrate varieties of English. Chinua Achebe's *Morning Yet on Creation Day* would promote discussions of "world English," African English, and their uses in writing (1976).

In the freshman English course, communitas can be brought about through student and teacher dialogue over shared texts. To paraphrase Bruffee, when working collaboratively on reading and writing, what students do is converse:

> They talk about the subject and about the assignment. They talk through the writer's understanding of the subject. They converse about their own relationship and, in general, about relationships in an academic or intellectual context between students and teachers. Most of all they converse about and as a part of the writing. (1984, 645)

The university class could examine the composing processes of professional second-language writers. Interestingly, much of this composing is done collaboratively between native and nonnative writers. For example, Jerzy Kosinski, a novelist and a nonnative speaker of English, always composed collaboratively although both he and his collaborators were uneasy about the term and the ways in which it muddied the notion of individual authority. He worked closely with a native speaking "editor" who gave him feedback on his texts. One such editor "would take Kosinski's typed copy and, in the space between lines, write his own more florid version of it, often providing three or four word choices from which the author could make selections" (Schiff 1988, 169). At other times Kosinski would dictate and the editor would "take it down in longhand. This text would be typed up and the two would "go through it and [the editor] would make editorial suggestions and [Kosinski and the editor] would edit it together" (1988, 169). Kosinski also would ask people with other native languages, Spanish or German, to write out sentences for him and then he would try to see how they "would do things differently." Kosinski used collaboration to help him appropriate English and to write polyphonically. In his text, he wanted styles in conflict, that did not mix well, "a field of tension" between his language and that of his editors. Critic Jerome Klinkowitz recognized that "we haven't invented a word to describe what Koskinski does. It's not ghost writing. It's linguistic experiment" (1988, 168). Teachers would do well to encourage this quality of experimentation and collaboration in the composing processes of their nonnative speakers. For Koskinski, the value of composing "collaboratively" in another language was that "English, my stepmother tongue, offered me a sense of revelation, of fulfillment, of abandonment" (1988, 168).

University educators generally think that the freshman English course should teach students to write academic prose. There is little agreement about what "academic discourse" is, however, beyond the recognition that the discourses of the academy are many, and that they are all "ccrrect" English. If the term is to have any meaning, to be any type of a guide for the freshman English class, then we need to go beyond the acknowledgment of multiplicity and the stricture of standards, and look more closely at both the centrifugal and centripetal forces of this discourse. Together with their students, composition teachers can think carefully about the notion that they can and should write their texts alone in completely native-like prose. They can talk with academics who write in English as a second language, find out what their composing and editing processes are, and how they define standards of language for themselves, in their personal and professional varying literacy practices.

Coles and Wall argue that specific language acts distinguish academia:

> While this [academic discourse] community is far from homogeneous, it agrees to teach . . . : the ability to define abstract concepts, to generalize, to use exemplification and demonstration, to acknowledge other viewpoints, to ground authority on intellectual claims and to question and critique established authorities in a field of knowledge. (1987, 299)

Coles and Wall also claim that they agree to teach these language acts because they are "empowering to students" (1987, 299). If, however, we understand "empowerment" to mean an ability to question, and thus become an agent in, social formations, we need to establish priorities among the academic language acts we teach. We will, for example, want to teach definition not as a mimicking of received opinion but as an action that follows from acknowledging, questioning, and critiquing the points of view of others.

For the teacher who sets out to teach this version of academic discourse, the freshman English class would become an arena in which

> ingrained habits of making meaning both in the text and in the world, come under examination; and while the classroom still helps

to elaborate and refine perception, it no longer assumes that we all start with the same set of associations or commitments. Not only are interpretive techniques introduced here, but the meanings we each derive from them are examined. Reading becomes the study of how we make sense of things focused both on shared texts and on what we as individuals and as a group make of them. (Roemer 919)

Carried out in a sheltered space and time, this concentration on differences actually works to disrupt hierarchies. Within the social interactions of communitas, making meaning and examining the making of meaning calls into question the social loyalties of everyday life. The collaborative process of reading and writing texts creates communitas in which students can envision change.

Chapter Six

Great Expectations: Reading and Responding to ESL Student Writing

Readings of student texts are social processes. Our expectations for and habits of reading are produced through social relations that the readings themselves reproduce. When teachers read, their interpretations and experiences of the text are determined at least in part by the social stance they take toward the student. In the role of teacher, we may assume authority over the ESL student and her text. If we do, this authority allows us to appropriate the text, to assume we know what it means, what it doesn't mean, and what its language should be. In a classroom of communitas, teachers do not presume that their difference, their knowledge, and the hierarchy embedded in the institution gives them authority to appropriate student texts. Instead, negotiating meaning, they enter into dialogue with students about their texts. When we alter our relationships to our students, we will also read their prose in a more egalitarian way.

In this final chapter I question authoritative readings of student texts, responses that consistently and as a matter of course demoralize both instructors and students because they focus on a lack in student texts. I want to argue that by looking beyond error and evidence of language acquisition, ESL teachers and students could construct rich responses that are generous in meaning. Using the constructs of M. M. Bakhtin, in this chapter I will work on shaping a vocabulary for reading ESL writing with an ear for the heteroglossia, the many voices, selves, and cultures that each writer constructs. This vocabulary can help students and teachers to see how response involves talk, not only about language forms, but also about content, action, and changing social relationships between readers and writers.

I begin this chapter by discussing my research into how teachers read ESL student texts.[1] I began this research because I wanted to see if and how teachers' (tacit or conscious and explicit) theories about composing would influence their interpretations of their students' writing. Below, I discuss the reading processes of two ESL composition teachers who were not atypical of the group studied.[2] For this research, the teachers spoke aloud their thoughts while reading student papers. These monologues were taped. Then as the teachers listened to the tape, I asked them to elaborate on elliptical comments. Finally, together the teachers and I wrote a text which represents both their reading processes and their commentary on their reading processes. In presenting these reading process texts, I do not in any way claim that they serve as direct evidence of cognition. The accounts are necessarily interpretive and partial.

Yet, the teachers all agreed that the texts do reveal important contours of their reading processes. Even if they had spoken aloud only the aspects of the reading process that they judged to be relevant to me or some other hypothetical audience, their comments represented what they perceived to be the values to the ESL/composition teacher and researcher community. If they were censoring their commentary, in other words, then certainly they spoke aloud only what they thought would be appreciated by the researcher, which is significant in itself.

In the following excerpts from teacher protocols in the first person, the "I" refers to the teacher, even though the text was written collaboratively by me and the teachers who were part of the study. When the texts were completed and the teachers had carefully considered the final drafts, they agreed that these accounts represented important aspects, perhaps even the core, of their reading processes for ESL student writing. They also felt that after having participated in this study, they read student papers differently, more generously, than they had before. One teacher remarked that prior to examining his reading processes, he had been responding to "only part of the text."

Teacher One: Excerpts from Protocol

These were the first papers of the semester. In groups the students had revised and edited their work. I was no longer concerned about making comments so that students could revise these papers further.

I really was more interested in evaluation than anything else at this point. I began my reading with this paper because it was on the top of the stack.

Student Paper A: "Las Vegas"

Las Vegas is a very well know city to everyone. It is very well known for its casinos, shows and overall it is a well known place for having fun. You can get rich in a matter of few hours, and you can get poor in a matter of few hours, if you are not on lock.

I had heared and seen alote about Las Vegas in T.V. , but I had never been there until last summer. I could hardly wait to get there while we were driving to there from L.A., finally after 5 hours of driving the city was visible from the freeway. We took Las Vegas Blvd. exit and intered the city. Since it was night the lights of the casinos were on, and I could not feel the darkness of the night.

I was very much amazed seeing that many casinos all at one place. We entered the drive way of the hotel which we were going to stay for the time that we were in Las Vegas. I went to the lobby of the hotel; the sound of the Jackpots, people, and the winners could be very well heared. These noises directed me to the casinos door. I was very much excited, but at the same time I was worried to enter the casino because I was under age. I decided to walk into the casino, and pretend everything is normal. I entered the casino and could see people playing blackJack, Poker, Jackpot, and rollet. The place was very crowded. While I was walking in the casino, every second I was waiting for someone to come and ask me to leave, but thanks to God this never happened.

I had a high fever for playing. I got some tokens and started playing rollet, right away.

(Teacher One: Protocol Continued)

The paper begins *"Las Vegas is a very well know city to everyone."* I wonder where they get those introductory sentences. This one looks awfully familiar, maybe because of the "everyone." I remember all those papers which begin "every country in the world." Do Arabic speakers have a tendency to do this more than other students? Maybe this is some kind of standard formulaic opening, some interference from Arabic rhetoric?

"It is very well known for its casinos, shows, and overall it is a well known place for having fun. You can get rich in matter of few hours, and you can get poor in matter of few hours, if you are not on lock." I wonder if this is also transferred from Arabic which requires repetition and redundancy in effective persuasion. Is the writer aware that he is doing this? Is this his intention, or is he avoiding other forms in English? What does he mean by "on lock." Is this a

translation? No. I get it, he means "in luck," an error with the preposition and a typo account for this problem.

I read on. The next paragraph reads nicely, better than the first. I note *heared* and *alote*, but when I get to *in T.V.* I translate the *in* to *on*. In line 6 and 7 the *while we were driving* stops me; I am confused. I reread the whole line to understand what is going on. I decide it is the order of the information which confused me and not, strictly speaking, any grammar error and I move on. In line 8, I note *intered*, reread the sentence and translate this word to *entered*. Lines 9–10 I enjoy, especially after the *and* it has a nice sound. The image is common, yet I appreciate the sentence.

In the next paragraph, I stop at line 12. To understand the sentence I do not have to reread it. Nonetheless, I reread the sentence and note that the word *which* is a problem. I read the sentence again, and I substitute *where* for *which*. I am surprised that this writer still has not learned to handle this distinction correctly. From the rest of his writing, it seems that he would be beyond this point. I wonder how many others in the class will have this problem. I could do a lesson on it. I feel pleased reading *the sound of the Jackpots, people,* ... (line 13–14) until I hit *I could heared*. It falls flat. I am disappointed. I wonder if he achieves the nice phrases by accident. I skip around now. In the last sentence (not excerpted) I notice a phrase *what it mattered was.* ... This is a fairly sophisticated structure but the pronoun use belies his control again. ...

Teacher Two: Excerpts from Protocol

Usually, I try to read a set of student papers—that is, the work of an entire class on a given assignment, in one sitting. I may or may not try to respond to or comment on them at this time. Usually, I make this decision after I have read several texts. A sense of what I want to do with the papers develops as I proceed; the group of papers forms a separate text to which I am responding. I form two images simultaneously, that of a particular paper and that of the class as a whole. My responses to the class formulate themselves in pedagogical terms; they lead to ideas for other writing assignments or class discussions. On a first reading, my reaction to an individual paper only influences the manner in which I will comment on the paper to the student. From my first impression of a student's text, I develop an attitude, which in a subsequent reading, will structure my approach to the paper. For example, I may remember that Kai Chan's writing about his trip to China was extremely interesting. Yet I have a recollection that his control of syntax is minimal. When I read his paper the second time, I read only for those errors which he could be trained to edit out. Because my initial response (and memory of this response) was so positive, I adjust my second reading accordingly; there is no point in worrying about all of the odd prepositions, for example, when he can communicate so effectively in written English.

I will read this paper first. It is written by a Chinese woman from Singapore. She wears boots and has purple streaks in her hair. I hope that the essay will be funny. The writer is funny, an odd sense of humor.

Student Paper B: "The Plug Hole"

Two rocky foot-paths are leading into a woodland which gives everybody an impression of wetness and darkness. Tall trees are growing everywhere, standing silently, watching patiently everything below them. The whole place is covered with grasses and a considerable amount of brushes. Dry leaves and broken branches are scattered all over the place. Sometimes, one can see some small yellow daisies and other unknown tiny flowers, surviving bravely between all the other plants. There are various species of birds, living in the woodland, making their nests on their favourite trees. They like to travel, but after all, singing is their real talent. The most annoying insects in the wood are the flies which love to attack who ever passes by the area. Squirrels are the characteristic animals of the woodland. They are always full of energy, jumping from one tree to another or climbing up and down the trees. They can certainly represent the active portion of the woodland. Bees and butterflies are the most hard-working insects. They fly from flowers to flowers, collecting nectar for food. All these are belonged to the woodland. There is no doubt about it. The thing which should not be there are the cigarette ends, lying on the ground, behind the brushes.

The woodland was nicked name the "Plug Hole". It is next to the boarding house, outside of my old school ground, in England. More precisely, it is at one of the school entrance where a main road is going into the school. And on the side of the road, there are two rocky foot-paths perpendicular to the main road, leading down to the "Plug Hole." It is not included in the school properties. It is opened to the public and therefor, no girls of Talbot Heath are allowed to go down there. The most important characteristic feature of the plug hole is that nobody can see clearly what is happening down there from either the school area or the main road, except when they try to look very carefully. Even when cars going out or entering the school entrance cannot see whether somebody are down there. It is definitely a good place to hide, smoke, meeting foreigners such as boyfriends and also to hold a secret meeting, etc.

I started to know this place when I first picked up smoking. My roommate, Sue, who smoked like a chimney. We visited the "Plug

Hole very often, about twice a day, saying our house-mistress that we were very desperate for a walk after our meals. Sometimes, we went in a crowd of five or even up to eight girls. We went there no matter what the weather was like: rainy, sunny, windy, snowy and foggy.

Sometimes, I went there alone during the week-ends when my friends were away or on exits. I usually sat on the grass smoking, day-dreaming and wondering what was the possibility that we were allowed to smoke in the boarding houses.

I remember one sunday morning, after church, I went down there with my friend Mandy. We were sitting there smoking. Suddenly snows were falling heavily. We did not move or talk, just sitting there, trying to cover our cigarettes from the snows. When we looked up, both of us were already covered with snows, all our clothes and hair. We stared at each other for a while and immediately both of us burst into laughter at the same time. This was really an interesting experience to me. Also at one time, after I went to the "Plug Hole," I could not find my ankle brace which was very precious to me. With no second throught, I traced all the way to the "Plug Hole," looking for my ankle brace in danger, worrying that I might be caught. I looked through everywhere in the "Plug Hole", but I still could not find it. After two weeks, I accidentally found my ankle brace, hiding in one of the side pocket of my school over-coat. This really had taught me a lesson on looking after my properties carefully.

To me, the "Plug Hole" was not only a place for secret activities, but also a place to go when I felt bored, upset or depressed. I felt fresh there where I could breath in some woodland smell. I loved wandering along the rocky foot-path, imaging that I would like to become a bird flying in the sky or a squirrel climbing the trees. I remember, once, I was scared by a squirrel which made some unfamiliar sound which I thought it was somebody, inspecting me. All I did, was jumping into one of the brushes, hiding myself as quickly as I could. When I think about it now, it was scary but exciting.

Another time, when Caroline, Mandy, Sue and I were smoking and chatting our ways in the "Plug Hole." We suddenly say our head-mistress car, passing by, and stopping on the main road. We were so afraid that we flew our cigarettes in all directions and jumped quickly and swiftly into brushes like rabbits, jumping into their holes when chased by some fierce animals. "Plug Hole" was also an ideal place to communicate with my friends. Usually, when we were smoking there, we brought up some very interesting topics to talk about. And we often ended in some funny, rediculous conclusions.

Two weeks before I graduated from Talbot Heath. I knew that I would leave that school forever and also the "Plug Hole." I felt that I was going to miss something, especially the chatters, the laughters and the cigarettes in the "Plug Hole." The last time I visited the

"Plug Hole" before the day I left Talbot Heath. It was in the evening, I proposely went there on my own. I felt that I loved to be caught by somebody, so that I could tell her all about it. I told the "Plug Hole" that that was my last chance to smoke there and I wish that it would remain there and give Talbot Heath girls who are desparate for cigarettes a place to smoke. I realized that I would miss that place and surely that is true now. I love to visit the "Plug Hole" again and smoke under pressure.

(Teacher Two: Protocol Continued)

In line 1, I notice *are leading*. It is possible, I suppose, that she is writing in this tense deliberately. I skip to the next sentence to check the verb. Yes, it is also in the present progressive. I wonder if she intends this stylistic effect, or if she simply is confused about the use of this aspect. Grammar books always confuse students about this tense. In line three I am startled by the *standing silently, watching patiently*. Hmmmmm, parallel structure, the writer has a lot of control, so I suppose that she could have intended the effect in the first line. In line 7, I react to *surviving bravely*, ugh, how soppy. Is she being sarcastic, I wonder. *Favourite* is a clue to her education in English (line 9). I skim the rest of the page looking for other clues. I find one, actually more of an answer than a clue, in lines 20 and 21. She went to school in England, a boarding school no less. Well, perhaps that accounts for her air of self confidence in the class.

I go back to the first paragraph and pick up line 9. From this point until line 18, I am perplexed by the tone, trying to figure out what she intended: lyricism, humor, sarcasm? I am sick of the phrase *in the woodland*. Then in line 16 I notice the verb *are belonged*. Does she think this is passive, or an adjective? Is it hypercorrection?

In paragraph two, while reading the first sentence I momentarily get lost in the paper itself. I lose the self-consciousness of my role as "teacher reading student paper." I want to know more about the "Plug Hole." I begin to think of the Plug-Hole type places in my own life. This doesn't last long, however. I get caught by the "is going." Here the present progressive doesn't work at all. Now I doubt that she intended the first uses of it in lines 1 and 3.

This paper is interesting. Even though she spent all that time in England, at a boarding school with Heath in the name no less, you can still tell that she is a nonnative speaker. I wonder if there is any hope for her count/non-count noun problems. I should conference with her on this in my office, or send her to the writing center. I wonder who is available to work with her. We'll just have to work on these little problems. I wonder how fossilized they are. She seems bright and hard-working; I hope she catches on faster than my fossilized student last semester who didn't ever get anything, no matter how many times I explained what she was supposed to do. Maybe by the end of the semester she'll write better—I'll see less of the "snows" type of problem. Practice makes perfect—don't they say.

Analysis of Reading Protocols

These teachers said they read for meaning. But mostly they read for error. They grimaced at the language, acted as if they had been confronted and even repugned by sentences that displayed deviant, non-native syntax and lexicon. The reader of the "Plug Hole" responded harshly to the student text, saying that she was "sick of the phrase 'in the woodland.' " The reader of "Las Vegas" translated the prose into his own words, not only when he didn't understand (on lock), but also when the words simply did not match the ways that he would have constructed the sentences. He rewrites a *which* to a *where* without wondering about what the writer meant. To the degree that the teachers did read for meaning, they tried to make the student texts fit templates of their own meanings and language.

During most of their responses, these readers focused on analyzing the causes of error—whether the error resulted from first language interference or not, whether the student had actually ever learned the form or not, whether the student would benefit from instruction on language forms or not. Although it may have become naturalized to teachers, this is a very strange way to read texts: The reader approaches the text not to see, hear, and know what is there, but rather to perceive what isn't there. Put in other terms, the reader experiences what is there as not there because it isn't what the reader would have put there. The readers above may or may not have been very sophisticated and precise in their analysis of the errors and in their use of contrastive rhetoric, but even if they could have been more astute at error analysis, my point would not change; when they read, they assumed the authority to change the student's text, to correct it. They acted as though their readings *should* fix and ameliorate.

The students' authority and intentions were called into question by their language. The first reader wonders whether the writer "achieves nice phrases by accident," as though other writers always come up with "nice" phrasing not by accident. The second reader likes the effect of the progressive in *are leading*. Yet this reader holds her enjoyment and approval in abeyance as she searches for clues as to whether the author intended this effect. When she discovers another progressive that does not have the same pleasant effect, the reader decides that the writer could not have intended the first, and she withholds her approval of and involvement in the text. Her role as teacher/reader makes her judge the text before experiencing it; her judgment becomes her entire experience of the text.

In these readings, the form of the writing became its total content. Neither reader comments much on any other dimension of the pieces. There is nothing on theme or emotion, unity and disunity, effectiveness and power, ideas, images, tone, mood, tensions, contrasts and potential contradictions, perceptions about culture and ideology, metaphor, rhetoric, audience, purpose. The focus on structure remains at a very low level, morphemes and syntax. The second reader ignores a higher level of structure—what motivates and moves the piece from mystery to freedom, escape from school to a sudden nostalgia in which even the Plug Hole itself is contained in the school memories. The readers' comments are fragmented, on detail, on language, on error, each disconnected from the other.

Interestingly, the second reader begins all of her judgments with phrases such as "I wonder"; "It is possible"; "I suppose"; "perhaps." The reader is trying to acknowledge the writer's role in the making of meaning, to grant the writer some measure of authority. Simultaneously, and in contrast, the reader is moved to control the text (and the writer?) by analyzing its errors and prescribing treatment for them.

The teachers discussed above are not narrow-minded, vicious, or even deliberately authoritative. They responded to texts as they did because of their training, which defines literacy as personal, individual, and linguistic, blocking from vision the social construction and political implications of literacy practices. These teachers equate language, discourse, and text with structure. The structure(s) they consider may extend beyond the sentence into discourse cohesion or even into the "macro-structures" of a text. They may try to think about text in "interactivist" terms, but ultimately they tend to reify interaction into structures. For them, meaning is not *the interaction* between writer and reader mediated by text. Instead, a fixed meaning is *in the structures* of the text, and student readers need to be taught how to get this meaning out of it.[3]

Not only does language equal structure, but the structures of a language are known and fixed. When someone speaks or writes, it is a clear cut, black- and-white matter as to whether the syntax is correct, and whether the English is good or not. There is little sense that correctness is a relative judgment, a decision made in a context. What is to be said, for example, about the sentence "I had a high fever for playing" from the "Las Vegas" essay above? Is it incorrect? If so, how would one describe its error? What "should" it be instead? These readings emphasize the "inertia" and the "calcification" of language, "the degree to which [English] is hard-edged, a thing in its own right." The judgments point out "the impermissibility of any free stylistic development in relation to [English]" (Bakhtin 1981, 344). With this quite common attitude toward language, students cannot represent English; they must receive it, intact, "hard-edged," impermeable.

Reading, Response, and Heteroglossia

Michael Holquist, an interpreter of Bakhtin in English, argues against superficial understandings of his subject's work: "In such hasty appropriations it is all too clear that previous reading habits have not been changed." Conversely, he emphasizes that "An immersion in Bakhtin's thought will indeed *transform the way one reads* . . ." (1990, 108, emphasis added). This chapter calls for a transformation of readings based on a Bakhtinian philosophy of language.

First in importance to our purposes here is the way in which Bakhtin problematizes a "unitary" view of language:

> Philosophy of language, linguistics and stylistics (i.e., such as they have come down to us) have all postulated a simple and unmediated relation of the speaker to his *unitary and singular "own"* language, and have postulated as well a simple realization of this language in the monologic utterance of the individual. Such disciplines actually know only two poles in the life of language, between which are located all the linguistic and stylistic phenomena they know: on the one hand, the system of a *unitary language*, and on the other, *the individual* speaking in this language. (1981, 269)

As implied above, linguistics, the discipline in which most ESL teachers are trained, assumes that each individual possesses, as property, almost as part of the body, *a* language, as if it were a substance inside the body. This language itself is a hermetic, self-sufficient system. Conversely, Bakhtin calls for the recognition of tentativeness of a language; it is posited rather than given. A language achieves a center through an always uneasy stability between centrifugal and centripetal forces. The "centrifugal" forces of language work toward its "decentralization and disunification" (1981, 272). In this highly social view of language, the basic unit of language is the utterance, yet the utterance can never stand alone. It is always in dialogue. It is a response, and it calls for response. The concept of the utterance reflects and ensures the idea that all language is fundamentally social (1981, 272). The utterance is heteroglossic. All language is full of many languages. In Bakhtin's terms, the utterance "not only answers the requirements of its own language as an individualized embodiment of a speech act, but it answers the requirements of heteroglossia as well; it is in fact an active participant in speech diversity" (272). Both the social forces that produce heteroglossia and the heteroglossia itself of "The Plug Hole's" language put centrifugal pressures on "English." At the very least, utterances of "The Plug Hole" are inscribed in American standard academic English, American college slang of the late 1980s, British boarding school slang of the 1970s, standard British English, and foreign student English. These varieties of English result from social forces such as immigration, colonialism, industrialism, and so forth.

This "heteroglossia" exists alongside "centripetal forces," which "[impose] specific limits to it." Heteroglossia will not lead to solipsism and isolation. Communication is ensured *because* heteroglossia exists alongside centripetal forces, such as schooling, which "[crystalize language] into a real although relative unity" (1981, 270).

For Bakhtin, a language occurs through the social interaction of discourse. It is always a shared phenomenon:

> As a living, socio-ideological concrete thing, as heteroglot opinion, language, for the individual consciousness, lies on the borderline between oneself and the other. The word in language is half someone else's. It becomes "one's own" only when the speaker populates it with his own intention, his own accent, when he appropriates the word, adapting it to his own semantic and expressive intention. Prior to this moment of appropriation, the word does not exist in a neutral and impersonal language (it is not, after all, out of a dictionary that the speaker gets his words!), but rather it exists in other people's mouths, in other people's contexts, serving other people's intentions: it is from there that one must take the word, and make it one's own. (1981, 294)

When language is conceived in this way, reading and writing are acts which do more than seek a center, a norm; they also engage in dialogue about encounters of cultures; they live out difference, contradiction, and contrast. To reiterate, language acquisition is not simply a process of learning (or acquiring) the rules of a language, for the very notion of "a language" is problematized.

In reading student texts, teachers need to recognize this tension between the fixedness of a language and its fluidity. From this perspective, whether a feature is or is not an error—is or is not English— is not quite so easily determined. Beginning with the understanding of language as heteroglossic utterance, can we securely label the verb *are leading* an error ("The Plug Hole," line 1)? What about the language of this sentence, also from "The Plug Hole": "Squirrels are the characteristic animals of the woodland." Is the article in any sense an error? In addition, when we read these texts for their heteroglossia, for their many voices, we are no longer confined to reading the writing of nonnative speakers for what it isn't or for what it lacks. What we gain is a "whole series of phenomena" which were formerly "beyond [our] conceptual horizon" (Dialogic Imagination 269). As Colin MacCabe argues:

> Whereas for two centuries we exported our language and our customs in hot pursuit of the acquisition of raw materials and fresh markets, we now find that our language and customs are returned to us but altered so that they can be used by others. And alteration finds so (sic) that our own language and culture discover new possibilities and fresh contradictions. (1988,12)

Bakhtin helps to elaborate how these "new possibilities and fresh contradictions" are enacted:

> A meaning only reveals its depth once it has encountered and come into contact with another, foreign meaning: they engage in a kind of dialogue, which surmounts the closedness and one-sideness of these particular meanings for these cultures. We raise new questions for a foreign culture, ones that it did not raise itself; we seek answers to our own questions in it; and the foreign culture responds to us by revealing to us its new aspects and new semantic depths. Such a dialogic encounter of two cultures does not result in merging or mixing. Each retains its own unity and open totality, but they are mutually enriched. (1986, 7)

ESL texts raise new questions for American/British culture. Their interlanguage results from more than linguistic "interference" and "negative and positive transferences." In the first long paragraph of "The Plug Hole," the language is accented, foreign. The language suggests issues for discussion, many questions which the student may not have intended to pose. For example, I find that the foreign accent of the first long paragraph leads me to questions the Disney-like personification of animals and trees "in the woodland." The words assert while the accent denies the naturalness, the seamlessness of Bambi, Thumper, Flower, and the rest. The language of this first paragraph makes me self-conscious about and unsure of the values implicit in the forests of Disneyland. Or, in the "Las Vegas" piece, I am confronted with "get rich quick, get poor quick" cliches. The coming of age in America is symbolized by the journey to Las Vegas, the buying of tokens, and the "fever" of the games. The foreign tones highlight the ideologies; in heteroglossia, the beliefs that underpin Las Vegas (both the place and the piece of writing) are exposed and they unravel fast.

When talk about texts and language emphasizes contradictions and new possibilities—disunification, heteroglossia, and diversity—

the notion of error is suppressed. Accordingly, this discussion may invite the fear of Babel, apprehensions that are typically expressed in questions such as: What will happen to our students if we don't concentrate on correct English in the ESL literacy class? How can we allow students to write and read their own versions of English? Will they not create gibberish? Who will hire them? How can we give them a degree from an American university when they write "like that"? These questions are motivated by more than a concern for student welfare. These questions, read through the myth of Babel itself, represent both a quest for power over and the totalizing yet utopian desire to engulf the Other so as to eliminate difference, for once and for all. As teachers, our fascination and obsession with error reveals, or perhaps all too often conceals, our own involvement in the dialectics of ethnicity and universality.

ESL literacy practices propel both nonnative writers and native speakers who read their texts into an encounter with the Other. In describing first world reader responses to third world texts, Fredric Jameson theorizes about the experience of the Other that is mediated by texts:

> We sense between ourselves and this alien text, the presence of another reader, of the Other reader. . . . The fear and resistance I'm evoking has to do then with the sense of our own non-coincidence with that Other reader, so different from ourselves; our sense that to coincide in any adequate way with that Other "ideal" reader—that is to say to read this text adequately—we would have to give up a great deal that is individually precious to us and acknowledge an existence and a situation unfamiliar and therefore frightening—one that we do not know and prefer not to know. (1986, 66)

Through the act of reading, teachers can make the ESL student into an Other. When readers experience language which differs from their own, they my also find a profound chasm between themselves and the writers. The reader of the "Las Vegas" paper says in response to the first sentence of the piece "I wonder where *they* get *those* introductory sentences." Immediately, on contact with the foreignness of the language, the reader has made a *they* of the student writer. The reader fears not the individual writer per se, but "them," the mass of other writers and other readers who seem to repell "us" with their language. When teachers respond with emotions of hostility or perhaps despair to ESL students' texts and their differences, they create an us/them relationship between themselves and their students.

To read with fear, disappointment, and suspicion—to name a few of the emotions that arise out of differences—is not the ESL teacher's only option. The ESL literacy class can promote the dialogue of meanings which Bakhtin describes. Rather than quest for the right answer and (the sentence without error) in the processes of communitas, teachers and students can read texts so as to value questions, conflicts, and contradictions.

Rather than adopt the attitude that ESL student texts are unique in the problems they present for a reader, we can consider texts of all sorts as placed on a continuum of stability in which instability, intelligibility, and unintelligibility, depend on the context of the reading. The language of a physics textbook is undecipherable to an English professor. The structure and language of a poststructuralist novel is unintelligible to my friend who loves Dickens but has no training in the theory that informs the literature of post-structuralism. We gain much in meaning if we are willing to grant that ESL student texts are like many other texts in that they create problems of intelligibility for their readers.

These instabilities are points of interest. They are the places in which the text can teach, giving an experience of multiculturalism, when readers listen to and participate in the dialogue between (among) cultures. Reading for heteroglossia, we can share the experience of living in two languages. This type of reading levels differences among readers and writers. In this leveling, the text mediates communitas (through a particular reader and her reading), rather than the structure of social stratification that ensues from teachers' readings which look only or primarily for evidence of error or correct English. Sometimes the ESL student text is so unintelligible, so unstable that the reader feels totally alienated from it. Struggling with this text can teach us about how ESL literacy, and relationships mediated by ESL literacy isolate and confuse the writer. This text can help us understand the writer's experience and language. Most often, however, these texts are intelligible, and we can read to understand the ESL students' meaning. While we respond to this meaning, a moment of "universalism" occurs, with heteroglossia as the chosen tongue.

Our readings can segregate students from ourselves; we can create hostility and suspicion. Or we can examine and humanize our relationships to them and them to us. Through this process it is not only we who learn, but students whose ideas, language, and texts are respected and taken seriously in this way learn about their language(s) and about readers' responses to them. And, as a result, these students are better prepared to make choices about language.

Below, for the remainder of this chapter, I will illustrate some heteroglossic readings of ESL student texts. I do not mean that the students necessarily intended or even would agree with these interpretations of their writings. I am suggesting that heteroglossia creates the occasion for questions, problems, and issues that are interesting for students and teacher alike. These interpretations are open ended and partial. They are meant to illustrate that teachers and students can derive enormous richness by reading ESL student writing for its dialogues of voices—for the conflicts and contradictions of meanings—and for its ever-evolving dynamics of ethnicity and universalism. The interpretations highlight the students' working through their relationships to the Other and their new identities through the different voices in their texts.

Student Paper 1

This text is an excerpt of a piece written for an International Student Newsletter on a university campus. This excerpt is from an early draft of the text.

Student Text

Foreign Students' Problems in the U.S.

Education is very important because it improves human life. People always want to be improved to a better life and governments always want to reach the best technology. That is why most of governments send their students to the U.S. The United States is one of the most modern countries who has the best technology.

Studying outside your country is a very difficult situation. Once you leave your country you leave so many things behind. You will leave your family, friends, house, town, culture, language, food and others. When foreigners decide to come here their governments help them to get out but once they are here in the U.S. they have a lot of problems. Government's help abroad almost does not exist.

Interpretation

There are three voices in these paragraphs: the American and those of two foreign students. Throughout both the paragraphs, these voices shift and their varying perspectives enter into dialogue and conflict. As the conversation evolves, so do the relationships between the writer as author and the implied readers.

The paragraphs repeat conversations between the American and the foreign student. The first voice is that of the generic American, the Other, as constructed by the writer. This voice announces the cliche "Education is very important because it improves human life." Its stern and totalizing tone makes it nearly parodic of American ideologies of education and its value. The next sentence is the voice of the foreign student, recasting the statement, making it more personal with the word *people,* elaborating the remark by adding the concerns of governments. The responsibilities and pressures placed on the foreign student by her/his government hold the prose in place like iron shackles.

The sentence "People always want to be improved to a better life and governments always want to reach the best technology." may provoke the native-speaking reader to translate the phrasing into more idiomatic English; "People always want to be improved to a better life" is syntactically correct but not idiomatic. Native speaking Americans would probably rewrite it as: "People always want to improve their lives." or "People want a better life." In the original version, the passive voice indicates that something or someone will elevate or ameliorate the people themselves, and this somehow will also result in a better life. In the first rewrite, the people themselves are improving their lives (as though it is an entity somehow separate from them), and in the second, they are acquiring something which is better than the thing that preceded it. Here the reader's move to translate introduces a dialogue of meanings and values.

The phrase "That is why" is again the generic American. Here it sounds colloquial, a nearly phatic phrase that is followed by the foreign student's voice "most of governments send their students to the U.S.," again concerned about relations between students and governments.

The final sentence in the paragraph is once again a dialogue between the foreign student and the generic American. The American says, "The United States is one of the most modern countries," and the foreign student, unsure about this modernity and its worth and its values, writes "who has the best technology." The *who* leaves the reader unsure about whether technology defines modernity or adds to modernity; in either case it is an attribute about which the writer is ambivalent.

In the second paragraph, the first three sentences are in a third voice. This voice is also that of a foreign student. But this student voice differs from the one in the first paragraph; it is announced by the second person pronoun. The first foreign student voice creates the dynamics of ethnicity through the conflicting perspectives or values. The second foreign student includes the reader, whether teacher or other students, whether American or foreigner, in a *you* which borders on the universal. The next sentence "when foreigners decide to come here their governments help them to get out. . . ." is the voice of the American manifesting a dynamic of ethnicity which separates the "us" from the "them."

The paragraph concludes with the first foreign student voice, the student concerned with the pressure and the lack of assistance and compassion of either his own government or the United States.

These two paragraphs are rich in meanings. The first and the second paragraphs present conflicting pictures of education: the first suggests that education improves human life, the second that it can make you miserable because you have to give up family, home, culture . . . and the list goes on. The text also questions the role and attitude of the United States toward foreigners who "get out" and then "have a lot of problems." The phrase "get out" indicates collusion between the students and the United States, that the students have a reason to flee the home country. Immediately, though the students are rebuked when they actually get here and "have a lot of problems." Through the dialogic voices, this text exposes the dilemmas of foreign students. The reader also experiences the dynamics of ethnicity and universality in reading this text as the voices construct differing relations with the reader. The first foreign student opposes the generic American. The second foreign student voice suggests that the American could be something other than them.

I am not suggesting that teachers read or respond to all of every student text with such scrupulously fine-grained attention to language and the dialogues between voices. They do not need to sit at home alone, marking out a dialogue between textual voices. Instead, they could ask the students what they think. They could ask questions, pose problems, create teacher-student relationships that will result in the student trying to read the texts in this way. In short, they could teach students to hear the voices themselves. They could use a short reading like the one above to raise questions and encourage further revising and writing about: the relationships of governments to students, of home values to education in a foreign country, issues concerned with development and modernity, and the values associated with them by Americans. All very serious pertinent issues, worthy of much discussion between the teacher and the students, worthy of many other texts.

Student Paper 2

This next text was produced as an in-class writing in which the teacher had asked students to "use writing to think about the value of reading and writing, in English or in your native languages."

Student Text

In these days, people tend to avoid reading because we can get information through mass media more quickly and with less energy. But we must not forget the fact that reading and writing greatly contribute the prosperity of country. In highly developed countries, the rate of illiteracy is very low. On the other hand, it is very high in under developed countries. Many people there can communicate through speaking and listening each other. It seems no problem for communication. But there is the fact that they cannot communicate through letters. I don't know how it affects the development of their country. But I am sure that illiteracy hinders the development.

Reading and writing are crucial. I am also struggling to improve them. I know how hard it is to do that. Each person has special ability. Someone can write music, and the other can draw picture. It is evident that I have no ability to write music and draw good picture. It is no way to improve it. But writing and reading are different, I think. By making effort, I believe that I can improve someday.

Interpretation

This text is full of dialogue. The voices are unsure about literacy, its value, its meanings. The first voice is foreign: "In these days people tend to avoid reading." The second voice is the authoritative American, giving the reason "because we can get information through mass media more quickly and with less energy." An American ideology of efficiency rings throughout this statement about the reasons for avoiding reading. This voice makes a universalist move to include himself and all readers in the "we" that "avoids reading." Then it continues with the highly authoritative "we must not forget the fact that," only to be interrupted by a second foreign voice which says that "reading and writing greatly contribute the prosperity." Because of its foreignness, the phrase "contribute the prosperity" provokes the native speaker to ask what is meant; what exactly is the relationship between prosperity and reading and writing?

The authority rushes in with the answers, the facts: "In highly developed countries, the rate of illiteracy is very low. On the other hand, it is very high in under developed countries."

The first foreign voice returns to again explain that there is little need for literacy. "Many people there can communicate through speaking and listening each other. It seems no problem for communication." This was the voice to first point out that "people avoid reading." And yet again, the authority interjects "But, there is the

fact that . . ." To which the second foreign voice, the one muster-
ing support for literacy, replies "they cannot communicate through
letters."

Then an "I" voice of the ESL student grapples with this issue, "I
don't know how it affects the development of their country." And the
American authority voice cuts in with "But I am sure that illiteracy
hinders the development." Then someone says "Reading and writing
are crucial." This last sentence floats, raising the questions: who said
it, who believes it; crucial to what, to whom, how?

The student returns "I am also struggling to improve them." The
rest of the paragraph carries out a conversation about whether literacy is a talent, whether or not reading and writing are activities like
painting and composing music. The voice is tentative. This piece
reads like a debate, weighing the nature and value of literacy.

A dialogical interpretation of this student's text helps to illustrate conflicting perspectives on literacy and the ideology of literacy
in the United States. These conflicts and this ideology could be
explored further, perhaps periodically throughout a whole semester.
My point is that examining the form of the language in these pieces
leads to content—discussions about the value of literacy: why read,
why write; the relationship of literacy to development; the effect of
American university education on home values and culture; and so
forth—rather than to more discussions of form.

Student Papers 3 and 4

Last, I want to interpret two pieces of writing from a single student.
I hope thus to show how her range of voices and relationships
evolved across a semester.

Student Text:

How We Learn About Violence

Many people in the United States like to go to the theatre, pay some
money and whatch what they call "something real violent" they like
to see movies like "Rambo" and "Red October". They watch the
movie, they shout when their hero does something real dangerous.
After that, they go home and make coments about the big gun the
hero had or about all the kind of weapons they recognice.

Later on, when the news and other kind of programs come to
the television, these people sit ther to learn more about violence.
But they are not the only ones learning, their children are learning
too. These children whatch the same movies, or even if they are not
able to whatch those movies, they already have violence in the
cartoons. Cartoons with violence? Somebody can say that it is

imposible, but it is true. Many cartoons that American children are watching contain a lot of violence. How are Americans going to stop all this violence in the media. I don't really know and this is something that makes me sad.

Totally different is the way people in my country, El Salvador, learn about violence. There, a civil war has been going on for 11 years. there, You don't need to see "Rambo" in order to learn the different kind of weapons man is inventing. There, you see and hear the weapons close enough to understand that they are one of the most horrible things ever created.

There a child is ready to serve as a soldier if he is big enough to hold a gun. Childhood is not that easy as it can be here. Our children already know what a gun can do since they are able to pronunciate the word GUN.

Salvadoreans don't need protection from what they can see on television and theaters. Salvadoreans need protection from the fight that can start in the middle of the night and prohibit them to see the sun light next day, because they are already dead.

I think that we, the human being are crazy, we create what we don't have and when we already have it, we don't want it anymore. People in the United States are creating their own violence. Whereas people in El Salvador are trying to scape from it.

Interpretation

In this poignant piece, with a surprisingly universalist title "How We Learn About Violence," the voices create the Other and then negate it for a tentatively universalist "we." Through the many voices, the writer develops several relationships to Americans and to the people of her home country.

In the first two paragraphs, the American is the third person plural Other—"they" and "these people." At the end of the second paragraph the first person "I" voice speaks, commenting on the sadness of what "these people" are doing.

In the third paragraph the "I" voice continues, beginning to lecture to "you." The American is not quite as distant as in the first two paragraphs. The American is addressed, spoken to, not about, in phrases such as "You don't need to see Rambo. . . ."

Paragraphs four and five show how the subtext contradicts or at least questions the primary text of the piece, which seems to say that Americans and Salvadoreans are different. In the fourth paragraph, the writer places herself geographically close to the Americans with the word "here." Nevertheless, her very next word "our" refers not to an affiliation with the Americans but to a community with the Salvadoreans. Just as soon as the community of "our" is named it is negated in the fifth paragraph where the Salvadoreans rather than the Americans become "they."

The concluding paragraph is a whirlwind of relationships. It begins with the voice of the individual "I think that"; it continues to assert universalism rather boldly with "we, the human being . . . we create. . . ." The next sentence reintroduces social structure, locales and difference: "People in the United States are creating their own violence whereas people in El Salvador are trying to scape from it." The American ends as "they." El Salvador is not "they," but it is not "we" either. The "I" differentiates itself from both.

Late in the semester, this same writer was encouraged by the teacher "to try something unlike anything else you've written in the semester." The composition class was small, made of approximately two thirds native speakers of English and one third nonnative speakers. This piece was distributed to the whole class.

Student Text
An Interesting Class (Excerpted)

Let's to continue. THE CLASS. My classmates: I don't really know any of them; I didn't know any of them before I maybe I won't be able to know any of them either. But, I was able in this class to know what they think about specific topics. For example, do you remember when we were talking about homosexuality? do you remember that? Any way, I do remember, gee! what a fun I had. First at all, it was sure there were going to be some different opinions about it. But, my big surprise was to fine somebody who really reject any kind of relation with homosexual. He was really radical in his ideas. I think it is good to defend your position about something that strongly. Who was that person? (clew: D-E-R-R-I-C-K).

Let's pick up somebody else. (E-V-A), she was good when she ask about "my first kizz." I never told anybody, but my best friend about it, and there she was asking me to tell her what could I do? I had to write something. I must apologize to E-V-A, I am sorry E-V-A, I fool you; I didn't write the real thing. Whatever you read, was not the truth; I still keep my secret OK, who else? what do you say?, I didn't hear you, oh! . . . Who else? I know! N-A-T-A-S-H-A. She is nice and friendly . . .

OK, the next one and the last one is ME! Who am I? I am R-O-X-A-N-A.

What can I say about me. Personally, I think that I am not that bad student in this class. I try to speak whenever I can find the suitable words to express my point of view about something we are talking about. . . . That is enough, and anyway this is my last line in the paper so I should finish here. It is good to be in this class with you, I really enjoy it so much and what else? oh! IT IS NICE TO MEET YOU!

Interpretation

This is an astounding response to the teacher's prompt to "do something you have not yet done in writing." Bravely, this writer does do something she has not done. This student ends the semester working out her relations with her classmates, most of whom were American, in English. She tries to talk about knowing them and not knowing them. And then, she proceeds to try to get to know them better through the writing. She compliments, and she confesses. She ends by introducing herself.

Her language is energetic, casual, foreign, and young. She uses slang, exclamation marks, and whole words in capital letters. The voices of this text are not the serious lecturing voices of "How We Learn About Violence."

The language of the text seeks relationships similar to those developed through "How We Learn About Violence"; it replays the dialectics of ethnicity and universality quite closely. The writer starts out saying that she doesn't know "them." She might know what "they" think, but she doesn't "really know any of them." Abruptly, however, she addresses someone (of "them") directly, "For example, do *you* remember when *we* were talking. . . ." For a moment, with the word *we*, the writer invokes communitas. In recreating the class's polemical discussions of homosexuality, this writer creates community. Soon enough though, the *we* separates; Derrick becomes the third person *he*; Eva is *she*, and the writer is *I*. In the final excerpted paragraph, the writer is I and the class and the implied reader are *you*. She ends by introducing herself and speaking not *about* but *to* the reader who is her classmate(s). The student actually revised this text slightly and added a final short paragraph in Spanish in which she said good bye to the class, adding her hopes that the reader could understand her Spanish without having to use the dictionary too much. In this paragraph she addressed the reader as *you*, but in Spanish, thereby reproducing the dialectics of ethnicity and universality once again.

This text has enormous value in the relations that it is mediating.

Great Expectations

And what does this pedagogy do for ESL literacy students who must fulfill requirements and pass exams for degrees, for certificates, for amnesty, or for jobs? The students in Christina's class no longer worried about the English test at the foundry. Instead, as a group, they read and wrote and tried to get information not only about the test, but about breaks, about the heat, and about job security. The university ESL students talked to their chemistry, business, and psychology professors about language, their expectations, literacy, and exams. These students were better prepared to understand what was expected of them and to appropriate the word or to resist it, if necessary.

The pedagogy of communitas respects and even encourages the heterglossia in student texts. The many voices reflect and create new possibilities for social relationships and social interaction: through these voices we see that students use ESL literacy to protect the "we" of ethnicity, or like Roxana, they can use it to experience a "we" in the class with their classmates. As this "we" broadens, they may momentarily feel the "we" of universality, as expressed in a title or a single clause. When this "we" occurs in heteroglossia, it is not a hermetic, self-sufficient abstraction. Within the utterance are many voices, other community formations. In both writing and reading, ESL students and teachers alike acknowledge and appreciate differences among people and their languages. This is the sound of living communitas.

Notes

1. In this chapter the example student texts are taken from a variety of classes at the community college and university level. Teachers could certainly respond to texts from adult school classes in a Bakhtinian manner, as well. The subsequent activities and discussions that the teacher would develop with students would differ, of course, depending on student interests and needs.

2. The study involved reading protocols for ten ESL and composition instructors and five instructors of other disciplines.

3. For example, I find the work of ESL reading specialist Patricia Carrell confused on this point.

Works Cited

Achebe, Chinua. 1976. *Morning Yet On Creation Day*. Garden City, New York: Doubleday Anchor.

Afolayan, A. 1971. "Language and Sources of Amos Tutola." *Perspectives on African Literature*. Ed. Christopher Heywood, 49–61. London: Heinemann.

Anaya, Rudolfo. 1972. *Bless Me Ultima*. Berkeley, California: Tonatiuh International.

Ashton-Warner, Sylvia. 1963. *Teacher*. New York: Bantam.

Bailey, Richard. 1983. "Literacy in English: An International Perspective." *Literacy for Life*. Ed. Richard W. Bailey and Robin M. Fosheim, 30–42. New York: MLA.

Bakhtin, M. M. 1981. *The Dialogic Imagination*. Trans. Caryl Emerson and Michael Holquist. Ed. Michael Holquist. Austin: U of Texas P.

———. 1986. *Speech Genres & Other Late Essays*. Trans. Vern W. McGee. Ed. Caryl Emerson & Michael Holquist. Austin: U of Texas P.

Bell, Jill and Barbara Burnaby. 1984. *A Handbook for ESL Literacy*. Toronto: OISE Press.

Berthoff, Ann E. 1982. *Forming Thinking Writing: The Composing Imagination*. Portsmouth, NH: Boynton/Cook.

Bizzell, Patricia. 1986. "What Happens When Basic Writers Come to College." *College Composition and Communication* 37: 294–301.

Blanton, Linda. 1988. *Ideas Exchange: Books 1 & 2*. New York: Newbury House.

———. 1990. "Talking Adult Students into Writing: Building on Oral Fluency to Promote Literacy." National Clearinghouse on Literacy Education. August, 2.

Bloomfield, Leonard. 1933. *Language*. New York: Holt.

———. 1942. *Outline Guide for the Practical Study of Foreign Languages*. New York: Academy.

Boas, Franz. 1911. Introduction. *A Handbook of American Indian Languages*. Washington, D.C.: Smithsonian.

Bodman, Jean and Michael Lanzano. 1975. *No Hot Water Tonight*. New York: Collier.

Brandt, Deborah. 1990. *Literacy as Involvement: The Acts of Writers, Readers, and Texts*. Carbondale, Illinois: Southern Illinois UP.

Bruffee, Kenneth A. 1984. "Collaborative Learning and the Conversation of Mankind." *College English* 46: 635–52.

———. 1986. "Social Construction, Language, and the Authority of Knowledge: A Bibliographical Essay." *College English* 48: 773–90.

———. 1972. "The Way Out: A Critical Survey of Innovations in College Teaching with Special Reference to the December, 1971, Issue of *College English.*" *College English* 33: 457–70.

Bruner, Jerome. 1983. *In Search Of Mind: Essays in Autobiography.* New York: Harper.

Bulosan, Carlos. 1973. *America Is In The Heart.* Seattle: University of Washington Press.

Burke, Kenneth. 1961. *Attitudes Toward History.* Boston: Beacon.

———. 1962. *A Grammar of Motives and A Rhetoric of Motives.* New York: World.

Byrd, Donald R.H., and Gloria Gallingane. 1990. *Write Away 1.* New York: Newbury House.

Carrell, Patricia L. 1987. "Content and Formal Schemata in ESL Reading." *TESOL Quarterly* 21:461–81.

Chastain, Kenneth. 1976. *Developing Second Language Skills: Theory to Practice.* Chicago: Rand.

Chomsky, Noam. 1965. *Aspects of Syntax.* Cambridge: MIT Press.

———. 1966. *Cartesian Linguistics: A Chapter in the History of Rationalist Thought.* New York: Harper.

———. 1962. "Explanatory Models In Linguistics." *Logic, Methodology and Philosophy of Science.* Ed. E. Nagel, P. Suppes, and P. Tarksi. Palo Alto: Stanford UP.

———. 1980. *Language and Mind.* New York: Harcourt.

———. 1957. *Syntactic Structures.* The Hague: Mouton.

Cliff, Michelle. 1989. *No Telephone To Heaven.* New York: Random House.

Clifford, James. 1988. *The Predicament of Culture: Twentieth Century Ethnography, Literature and Art.* Cambridge: Harvard UP.

Coles, Nicholas, and Susan V. Wall. 1987. "Conflict and Power in the Reader-Responses of Basic Writers." *College English* 49: 298–314.

Cooper, Marilyn M., and Michael Holzman. 1989. *Writing As Social Action.* Portsmouth, NH: Boynton/Cook.

Connor, Ulla, and Robert B. Kaplan. Eds. 1987. *Writing Across Languages: Analysis of Second Language Text.* Reading, MA: Addison-Wesley.

Croft, Kenneth, ed. 1972. *Readings on English as a Second Language.* Cambridge: Winthrop.

Cummins, Jim. 1979. "Linguistic Interdependence and the Educational Development of Bilingual Children. Bilingual Education Paper Series 3/2. ERIC Document Reproduction Service No. ED 257 312.

Cummins, Marsha. 1982. "Group Activities for Non-Native Students in Regular Freshman English." *Non-Native and Nonstandard Dialect Students: Classroom Practices in Teaching English 1982–83.* Ed. Candy Carter, 44–46. Urbana, IL: NCTE.

Dalthorne, O.R. 1975. *African Literature in the Twentieth Century.* Oxford: Heinemann Educational Books.

Dasenbrock, Reed Way. 1987. "Intelligibility and Meaningfulness in Multicultural Literature in English." *PMLA* 102: 10–19.

Derrida, Jacques. 1974. *Of Grammatology.* Trans. Gayatri Spivak. Baltimore: Johns Hopkins UP.

———. 1985. *The Ear of the Other: Otobiography, Transference, Translation.* Trans. Peggy Kamuf. Ed. Christie V. McDonald. New York: Schocken.

Derwing, Bruce L. 1973. *Transformational Grammar as a Theory of Language Acquisition.* Cambridge: Cambridge UP.

Dulay, Heidi C., and Marina Burt. "You Can't Learn Without Goofing." Richards 95–123.

Dwyer, Carlota Cárdenas de. "Poetry." Leal 19–27.

Elsasser, Nan, and Vera John-Steiner. "An Interactionalist Approach to Advancing Literacy." Shor 45–62.

Emerson, Caryl. 1983. "The Outer Word and Inner Speech: Bakhtin, Vygotsky, and the Internalization of Language." *Critical Inquiry* 10: 245–64.

Emig, Janet. 1971. *The Composing Processes of Twelveth Graders.* Urbana, IL: NCTE.

Epstein, Jennifer L. 1985. "Teaching Vocational Literacy Skills to Refugees: How Do You Apply For A Job When You Have Never Held A Pencil?" *ERIC/CLL News Bulletin* 9: 5–8.

Fallis, Guadalupe Valdés. 1976. "Code-Switching in Bilingual Chicano Poetry." *Hispania* 59: 877–86.

Fiore, Kyle, and Nan Elsasser. "Strangers No More: A Liberatory Literacy Curriculum." Shor 87–103.

Fishman, Joshua. "Knowing, Using and Liking English as an Additional Language." Grabe n. pag.

Flower, L., and J. R. Hayes. 1981. "A Cognitive Process Theory of Writing." *College Composition and Communication* 32: 365–87.

Freedman, Aviva, et al., eds. 1983. *Learning to Write: First Language/Second Language.* New York: Longman.

Freire, Paulo. 1970. "The Adult Literacy Process as Cultural Action for Freedom." *Harvard Educational Review* 40: 363–81.

———. 1982. *Pedagogy of the Oppressed.* New York: Continuum.

Fries, Charles C. 1945. *Teaching and Learning English as a Foreign Language.* Ann Arbor: U of Michigan P.

Gardner, R. C., and W. E. Lambert. 1972. *Attitudes and Motivation in Second Language Learning.* Rowley: Newbury House.

Gates, Henry Louis, Jr. 1985. "Editor's Introduction: Writing 'Race' and the Difference It Makes." *Critical Inquiry* 12: 1–20.

Geertz, Clifford. 1973. *The Interpretation of Culture.* New York: Basic Books.

———. 1983. *Local Knowledge: Further Essays in Interpretive Anthropology.* New York: Basic Books.

Gerard, Albert S. 1971. *Four African Literatures.* Berkeley: U of California P.

Giles, H., ed. 1977. *Language, Ethnicity, and Intergroup Relations.* New York: Academic.

Gleason, H.A. 1955. *An Introduction to Descriptive Linguistics.* New York: Holt.

Goldstein, Lynn M. 1987. "Standard English: The Only Target for Nonnative Speakers of English?" *TESOL Quarterly* 21: 417–36.

Goody, Jack. 1977. *The Domestication of the Savage Mind* Cambridge: Cambridge UP.

Grabe, William, and Robert Kaplan, eds. 1980. *Prospect and Retrospect: An Introduction to Language Planning.* Unpub. MS 1980.

Halliday, M. A. K. 1975. *Learning How To Mean: Explorations in the Development of Language.* London: Edward Arnold.

Harder, Bernhard D. "Cultural Value Differences in the Stylistic Problems of English Compositions Written By Japanese Students." 25th International Conference of Orientalists, Tokyo, 1980.

Harris, P. R. 1970. "On the Interpretation of Generative Grammars." M.Sc. thesis. U of Alberta. 1970.

Hatch, Evelyn Marcussen. 1978. *Second Language Acquisition: A Book of Readings.* Rowley: Newbury House.

Harste, Jerome C., Virginia A. Woodward, and Carolyn L. Burke. 1984. *Language Stories and Literacy Lessons.* Portsmouth: Heinemann Educational Books.

Haugen, Einar. 1973. "The Curse of Babel." *Daedalus* 102: 47–56.

———. 1972. *The Ecology of Language.* Palo Alto: Stanford UP.

Heath, Shirley Brice. 1983. *Ways With Words.* Cambridge: Cambridge UP.

Hinds, John. "Reader versus Writer Responsibility: A New Typology." Connor 141–52.

The Hmong: Our Newest Neighbors. By Suzanne Smith. PBS. Sacramento. June 9, 1987.

Holquist, Michael. 1990. *Dialogism: Bakhtin and His World.* New York: Routledge.

Huebner, Thom. 1983. *The Acquisition of English: A Longitudinal Analysis.* Ann Arbor: Karoma Publishers.

Hymes, Dell. 1974. *Foundations in Sociolinguistics: An Ethnographic Approach.* Philadelphia: U of Pennsylvania P.

Hymes, Dell, and J. Frought. 1981. *American Structuralism*. The Hague: Mouton.

Jakobson, R. 1979. "The Twentieth Century in European and American Linguistics: Movements and Continuity." *The European Background of American Linguistics*. Ed. H. Hoenigswald. Dordrecht: Foris.

Jameson, Fredrik. 1986. "Third-World Literature in the Era of Multinational Capitalism." *Social Text* 15: 65–88.

Johns, Ann. 1981. "Necessary English: A Faculty Survey." TESOL Quarterly 15: 51–8.

Kaplan, Robert B. 1972. *The Anatomy of Rhetoric: Prolegomena to a Functional Theory of Rhetoric*. Philadelphia: The Center for Curriculum Development.

———. "Cultural Thought Patterns in Intercultural Education." Croft 245–62.

Karam, Francis X. "Literacy and Language Development." Grabe n. pag.

Kikimura, Akemi. 1981. *Through Harsh Winters*. Novato, California: Chandler and Sharp.

Kincaid, Jamaica. 1991. *Lucy*. New York: Plume.

Knoblauch, C.H., and Lil Brannon. 1983. "Writing as Learning Through the Curriculum." *College English* 45: 465–74.

Krashen, Stephen D. 1986. *Inquiries and Insights*. San Francisco: Alemany.

———. 1982. *Principles and Practices of Second Language Acquisition*. Oxford: Pergamon.

———. 1984. *Writing: Research, Theory and Applications*. Oxford: Pergamon.

Kroll, Barbara. 1978. "Sorting Out Writing Problems." *On TESOL '78: ESL Policies, Programs, Practices*. Ed. Charles H. Blatchford and Jacquelyn Schachter 176–82. Washington: TESOL.

Labov, William. 1972. *Sociolinguistic Patterns*. Philadelphia: U of Pennsylvania P.

Lado, Robert. 1964. *Language Teaching: A Scientific Approach* New York: McGraw-Hill.

———. 1957. *Linguistics Across Cultures: Applied Linguistics for Language Teachers*. Ann Arbor: U of Michigan P.

Lawrence Mary S. 1972. *Writing As A Thinking Process*. Ann Arbor: U of Michigan P.

Leal, Luis. et al, ed. 1982. *A Decade of Chicano Literature: Critical Essays and Bibliography*. Santa Barbara: Editorial La Causa.

Levins, Richard and Richard Lewontin. 1985. *The Dialectical Biologist*. Cambridge: Harvard UP.

Litwak, David. 1979. "Procedure: The Key to Developing an ESP Curriculum." *TESOL Quarterly* 13: 393.

Lomelí, Francisco. "Novel." Leal 29–38.

McLaughlin, Barry. 1987. *Theories of Second Language Acquisition*. Baltimore, MD: Edward Arnold.

McWilliams, Carey. 1973. Introduction. *America Is In The Heart*. By Bulosan, vii–xxiv. Seattle: U of Washington Press.

MacCabe, Colin. 1988. *Futures for English*. Manchester: Manchester UP.

Matalene, Carolyn. 1985. "Contrastive Rhetoric: An American Writing Teacher in China." *College English* 47: 789–808.

Méndez, Miguel M. "Interview." Bruce-Novoa 83–94.

Mendoza, Rita Urias. 1988. "Rape Report." Watershed 12: 1.

Murray, Donald M. 1978. "Internal Revision: A Process of Discovery." *Research on Composing*. Ed. C. Cooper and L. Odell. Urbana: NCTE.

Nemser, William. "Approximative Systems of Foreign Language Learners." Richards 55–63.

Ngara, Emmanuel. 1982. *Stylistic Criticism and the African Novel*. London: Heinemann.

Newmeyer, Frederick J. 1986. *The Politics of Linguistics*. Chicago: U of Chicago P.

Ngũgĩ wa, Thiong'o. 1986. *Decolonizing the Mind: The Politics of Language in African Literature*. London: James Currey.

Nishimura, Yoshitaro. 1979. "Japanese English: Its Sequence of Paragraphs." *Forum—Language and Literature* 4: 5–10.

Novoa-Bruce, Juan. 1980. *Chicano Authors: Inquiry by Interview*. Austin, Texas: U of Texas P.

———. 1982. *Chicano Poetry: A Response to Chaos*. Austin: U of Texas P.

Okara, Gabriel. 1973. "African Speech . . . English Words." *African Writers on African Writing*. Ed. G.D. Killam, 137–39. Evanston: Northwestern UP.

Olson, David. 1977. "From Utterance to Text: The Bias of Language in Speech and Writing." *Harvard Educational Review* 47: 257–81.

Ong, Walter. 1982. *Orality and Literacy*. London: Methuen.

Ostler, Shirley. "English in Parallels: A Comparison of English and Arabic Prose." Connor 169–85.

Peyton, Joy Kreeft. 1989. "Listening to Students' Voices: Educational Materials Written By and For LEP Adult Literacy Learners." National Clearing House on Literacy Education, December: 1–4.

Pierce, Bronwyn Norton. 1989. "Toward a Pedagogy of Possibility in the Teaching of English Internationally: People's English in South Africa." *TESOL Quarterly* 23: 401–20.

Pike, Eunice. 1977. "Historical Sketch." *The Summer Institute of Linguistics*. Ed. R. Brend and K. Pike, 21–39. The Hague: Mouton.

Pincus, Anita. 1964. "Structural Linguistics and Systematic Composition Teaching to Students of English as a Foreign Language." *English Language Teaching* 18: 185–94.

Povey, John. 1967. "Creative Writing in BIA Schools." *TESOL Quarterly* 1: 305–308.

———. 1969. "The English Language of the Contemporary African Novel." *Critique: Studies in Modern Fiction* 111: 79–96.

Pringle, Ian. 1985. "English Language, English Culture, English Teaching." *Language, Schooling and Society*. Ed. Stephen N. Tchudi, 119–132. Portsmouth, NH: Boynton/Cook.

Purdy, Dwight. 1986. "A Polemical History of Freshman Composition in Our Time." *College English* 48: 791–97.

Raimes, Ann. "Anguish as a Second Language?" Freedman 284–91.

———. 1985. "What Unskilled ESL Students Do as They Write: A Classroom Study of Composing." *TESOL Quarterly* 19: 229–58.

Rivera, Tomás. "Chicano Literature: The Establishment of Community." Leal 9–17.

Robinson, Jay L. 1985. "Literacy in the Department of English." *College English* 47: 482–98.

Roemer, Marjorie Godlin. 1987. "Which Reader's Response?" *College English* 49: 911–21.

Rodríguez, Richard. 1982. *Hunger of Memory*. New York: Bantam.

Rushdie, Salman. 1983. *Shame*. New York: Knopf.

Saldívar, Ramón. 1979. "A Dialectic of Difference: Toward a Theory of the Chicano Novel." *MELUS* 6: 73–92.

Sapir, Edward. 1931. "Conceptual Categories in Primitive Languages." *Science* 74: 578.

———. 1921. *Language*. New York: Harcourt.

———. 1949. *Culture, Language and Personality*. Berkeley: U of California P.

Saussure, Ferdinand de. *Course in General Linguistics*. Trans. Wade Baskin. Ed. Charles Bally and Albert Sechehaye. New York: Harcourt, 1966.

Schiff, Stephen. 1988. "The Kosinski Conundrum." *Vanity Fair* June: 115–70.

Schumann, John H. 1976. "Social Distance As A Factor in Second Language Acquisition." *Language Learning* 26: 135–43.

Scollon, Ron, and Suzanne Scollon. 1981. *Narrative, Literacy and Face in Interethnic Communication*. Norwood: Ablex.

Scribner, Sylvia, and Michael Cole. 1981. *The Psychology of Literacy*. Cambridge: Harvard UP.

Selinker, L. "Interlanguage." Richards 31–54.

Shor, Ira, Ed. 1987. *Freire for the Classroom. A Sourcebook for Liberatory Teaching*. Portsmouth, NH: Boynton/Cook.

Sifuentes, Roberto. "Essay." Leal 57–63.

Slager, William. "Classroom Techniques For Controlling Composition." Croft 232–44.

Slobin, Daniel. 1966. "Comments on 'Developmental Psycholinguistics'." *The Genesis of Language: A Psycholinguistic Approach.* Ed. F. Smith and G.A. Miller. Cambridge: MIT Press.

Smith, Frank. 1984. *Joining The Literacy Club.* Victoria: ABEL Press.

Smith, Phillip M., Howard Giles, and Miles Hewstone. 1980. "Sociolinguistics: A Social & Psychological Perspective." *The Social and Psychological Contexts of Language.* Ed. Robert N. St. Clair and Howard Giles, 283–98. Hillsdale: Erlbaum.

Steinberg, D. D. 1970. "Psychological Aspects of Chomsky's Competence-Performance Distinction." *Working Papers in Linguistics: University of Hawaii* 2: 180–92.

Steiner, George. 1975. *After Babel.* London: Oxford UP.

Street, Brian. 1984. *Literacy in Theory and Practice.* Cambridge: Cambridge UP.

Stuckey, Elspeth. 1991.*The Violence of Literacy.* Portsmouth, NH: Boynton/Cook.

Taylor, Barry P. 1981. "Content and Written Form: A Two-Way Street." *TESOL Quarterly* 15: 5–13.

Tuman, Myron. 1986. "From Astor Place to Kenyon Road: The NCTE and the Origins of English Studies." *College English* 48: 339–49.

Turner, Victor. 1986. *The Anthropology of Performance.* New York: PAJ Publishers.

———. 1974. *Dramas, Fields and Metaphors.* Ithaca: Cornell UP.

———. 1969. *The Ritual Process.* Ithaca: Cornell UP.

Tutuola, Amos. 1953. *The Palm-wine Drinkard.* New York: Grove Press.

Volosinov, V. N. 1973. *Marxism and the Philosophy of Language.* Trans. Ladislav Matejka. New York: Studies in Language, Vol. 1.

Von Humbolt, Wilhelm. 1971/1936. *Linguistic Variability and Intellectual Development.* Trans. George C. Buck and Frithjof A. Raven. Philadelphia: U of Pennsylvania P.

Vygotsky, L. S. 1981. "The Genesis of Higher Mental Functions." *The Concept of Activity in Soviet Psychology.* Ed. J.V. Wertsch, 163. New York: M.E. Sharp.

———. 1978. *Mind In Society.* Ed. Michael Cole et al. Cambridge: Harvard UP.

———. 1962. *Thought and Language.* Cambridge: MIT Press.

Wali, Obi. 1963. "The Dead End of African Literature." *Transition* 10: 93–107.

Wallerstein, Nina. "Problem-Posing Education: Freire's Method of Transformation." Shor 33–44.

Weinstein, Gail. 1984. "Literacy and Second Language Acquisition: Issues and Perspectives." *TESOL Quarterly* 18: 471–84.

Weinstein-Shr, Gail. 1989. "Breaking the Linguistic and Social Isolation of Refugee Elders." *TESOL Newsletter,* October: 9.

———. 1990. "Family and Intergenerational Literacy in Multilingual Families." National Clearinghouse on Literacy Education Q&A, August: 1–4.

Wertsch, James V. 1985. *Vygotsky and The Social Formation of Mind.* Cambridge: Harvard UP.

Whitney, Dwight. 1980/1875. *The Life and Growth of Language.* New York: Dover.

Whorf, Benjamin Lee. 1956. *Language, Thought and Reality.* Ed. John Carroll. Cambridge: MIT Press.

Widdowson, Henry. "New Starts and Different Kinds of Failure." Freedman 34–47.

Williams, Raymond. 1983. *Writing In Society.* London: Verso.

Zamel, Vivian. 1976. "Teaching Composition in the ESL Classroom: What We Can Learn From Research in the Teaching of English." *TESOL Quarterly* 10: 68–76.

———. 1982. "Writing: The Process of Discovering Meaning." *TESOL Quarterly* 16: 195–210.

Index